Small Town
Tales

Small Town Tales

A Brookline Boyhood

by

Sidney Hall, Jr.

[signature: Sidney Hall]

HOBBLEBUSH BOOKS

Published by HOBBLEBUSH BOOKS

Brookline, New Hampshire

Library of Congress Catalog Card Number: 97-93619

ISBN 0-9636413-3-6

Printed in the United States of America

8   7   6   5   4   3   2   1

The text of this book is composed in 12/14 Monotype Bulmer, with the display in Monotype Bulmer Display. Bulmer is based on types cut by William Martin, and used by the Printer, William Bulmer, circa 1790.

Acknowledgments

This book is a collection of the newspaper column, "A Brookline Boyhood," first published in the *Hollis/Brookline Journal* by Cabinet Press. "Uncle Elwood" and "The Big Baloney" also appeared in *Yankee Magazine*.

The cover photo shows the author (right) in 1962, with his father and two brothers.

The last chapter, "Where the Sweet Birds Sang," is indebted to Shakespeare's Sonnet #73.

Christmas 1997

To: Cody

enjoy

love, Nana & Gramps

for my father

*"I am certain of nothing
but of the holiness of the
Heart's affections and the
truth of Imagination."*

-Keats – letter, 1817

οὐ γάρ τι νῦν γε κἀχθές, ἀλλ᾽ ἀεί ποτε
ζῆ ταῦτα, κοὐδεις οἶδεν ἐξ ὅτου ᾽φάνη.

-Aeschylus

Not from any Now,
        but from Always,
these things live.

And no one knows
        from what place
                they shine.

(translated by the author)

Contents

Prologue

THERE IS A POINT AT WHICH the Atlantic Ocean carries herself proudly toward land and rages against the coastline not far from Boston. The breakers erupt against rock, trying to turn it to wood, sending the harsh, white spume rocketing skyward, then down like a shower of bullets into the hollows of cold stone. This violence doesn't know time. It was the same a year ago and ten years ago. It was the same 20 years ago. It was the same 32 years ago when I was a boy of thirteen. On a Monday morning in March of 1964, the fury was worse than ever.

Not far from the same cliff, on that Monday morning, the ocean opened herself to the majestic Merrimac. Upstream through the cities and towns of Massachusetts and New Hampshire, the Merrimac opened herself to the important Nashua. Further into New Hampshire the Nashua opened herself to the half-savage Nissitissit. In the center of my town of Brookline, the Nissitissit accepted waters from the Village Brook. Near the store, the brook flowed into and out of a fire hole. In the middle of the fire hole a bit of blue parka was floating in the icy March water. Underneath the parka was a small boy. The waves were pounding.

Earlier that same morning, our car bumped as my mother was backing it out of our barn. After lunch, my father got out a hoe to fill in the low spot. As he was working he heard the woman across the street calling for her son. He went over to help and learned that her three and a half year old boy, who was playing in the yard with their puppy only minutes before, had disappeared.

My father's brain worked quickly. He put two fingers to his mouth and whistled very loudly. In a moment the puppy trotted into view. He noticed that the dog's belly was wet, and without stopping to explain, ran full speed down Steam Mill Hill to the water hole above the store. The newspapers that later reported the incident included the fact that he was once a track star, to make the story better I suppose.

At the water hole, he saw small footprints leading out toward the middle, over what was left of the ice and snow. He spotted a bit of blue parka floating in the water. Somehow he jumped over a wire fence that was as tall as himself. He yelled for help, then swam toward the parka. He tried grabbing onto one of the floating ice pieces but it wouldn't hold him up. It was difficult to swim since he still had on his own parka and heavy boots. The boy was floating, so it was not hard to move him through the water to the bank.

He had learned something about "mouth to mouth" at fire meetings, and began on him immediately at the edge of the bank. A man came running to help and wrapped the boy in a blanket. The boy was not breathing. His eyes were locked way up and his jaw was clamped so tightly that my father could not get it apart, but he kept blowing air through the cracks in the boy's teeth. Others arrived and began to work the small chest.

A doctor arrived and gave the boy a shot in the arm and continued the resuscitation. The boy had not moved a muscle and had only apparently breathed one or two breaths. After a long time, the doctor concluded there was no hope. He was ready to pronounce the boy dead. My father, shaking with the cold, kept on anyway. After about 45 minutes, with everyone working together again, the boy was breathing freely. The next day the hospital listed him in good condition. Today he has his own children.

Most of us begin to shut down our brains and our hearts early in life and spend our days helping others toward a similar death. We don't mean to, and fight with ourselves over it. Some rare souls, like my father, never shut down either their brains or their hearts, and they spend their lives helping other people toward life.

When I came home from school that Monday and walked into our big upstairs bathroom, I found my father's clothes and the contents of his pockets and wallet laid out to dry. There were half a dozen notes with ink spreading like swollen brooks. There were wet unopened bandaids, a big ring of keys, a silver tape measure with a thumb print worn into its side, a pocket knife with paint on the black handle. I heard the whole story from my mother, thinking it was another good thing my father did, but not realizing, I think, how good a thing. "I guess that boy is alive today because the car bumped coming out of the barn in the morning," he wrote to his parents later in the week.

Twenty years later my father was upstairs in our house painting a big wooden door when his vision began to swim. He called out for help as he saw the ocean and saw the waves pounding violently on the rocks. He crumpled to the cold floor, even as he must have heard the frantic attempt to pull him back to shore, after one wave washed too high. No one could pull him back.

Small Town Tales

The Shedd Family

I GREW UP ON A BACK ROAD near the center of town (we had those then) in a roomy farmhouse that many years earlier had been the hub of a busy farm. The hillsides that now are woods were overlaid with apple and peach orchards. The peaches were some of the best in New Hampshire, or so my mother says. When I was a boy, a few samples of the old apple trees survived to spook us. The strange building across the street, where my father started a family business, had been a busy blacksmith shop, and another building had been the cooper shop. By the time I was born, there were only hints of this former life, and impressive stories of hard work. Our lives would be simpler, it seemed.

The Shedd family lived three telephone poles from us in another old farmhouse. Much of my childhood revolves about exploits, both clever and stupid, undertaken with members of the Shedd family. There were seven of them, just like my own family, and they were the quintessentially eccentric country family.

The high grass in the field behind the Shedd's house and behind our house was the site of dozens of childhood games; fox and geese, cowboys and Indians, cops and robbers, crab apple fights that lasted all afternoon, sometimes all weekend. At the bottom of the hill was Hall's Brook, which we dammed and swung across on ropes and used as a battle line in the crab apple wars. More than once we broke through its thin ice in the wintertime, three or four of us sitting in the freezing water on a long toboggan that had just come down the hill too fast. On the ball park side of the brook we had built a huge jump on the very steep hillside. We'd fly off it and land on our spines on completely flat ground before coasting into the brook.

There was a lot of abuse of our own bodies in those days, something the Shedd family encouraged, things like jumping out of second story barn doors, parachuting straight down through the cracking limbs of giant old pine trees, pummeling each other in unpublicized wrestling and boxing events in the woods, and on and on and on. I used to marvel, even at the time, that the human body could withstand so much.

Steam Mill Hill was the road in front of the Shedd's house. We used it all winter for sledding. There was a protracted time after snow storms when the hill was ideal for sliding. Cars came so infrequently, we didn't mind the occasional one coming to slide along with us.

One of our favorite games, invented apparently by the Shedds, and one that definitely fell into the "stupid" category, was playing "chicken" on our metal-runner sleds. One night I had just been run off the road by another sled and was lying on my back in the snow bank, when a third sled came down and ran diagonally across my leg. This hurt quite a bit, but it was so cold the pain soon vanished. I swung back up the hill for another run, but thought I'd better take a look at my leg first. When I rolled up my pants to the knee I found a big white bone glinting back at me in the dull moonlight. The Shedd family took me inside and put me on a couch with my leg up. The combination of thawing out, and hearing half a dozen kids repeat "Gawd, that must hurt!" really did make me start to hurt. I was taken to Doctor Crocker, in another town, who stitched the muscle back together and then the leg.

It made me a martyr of the incoming seventh grade class at the Junior High School in Nashua, the nearest city, where we went by bus to school. Since I was bound up in crutches for many weeks, my father instructed me not to waste a good opportunity. "Be sure only to ask the *girls* to carry your books," he said.

Flying

Mᵧ BEST FRIEND DAVID SHEDD at least had the prudence and the grace to tell me to bend my knees and crumple to the ground, or execute a roll, after I jumped from his second story barn door. Not everyone had adequate instructions before this rite of passage a small-town New England boy once had to go through on his way to bigger boyhood. People are under the mistaken impression that these hay doors were built for moving inanimate or inert country objects in and out of storage. They were really built for small boys to explore the possibilities of human flight.

Strange this solicitation from a member of a family that had, it seems, a broken leg, broken arm, fractured skull, black eye, cracked collarbone, or wrenched wrist making the rounds of the household (like the ghost of accidents past) for a good part of two decades.

It is amazing that my frail body sustained the shock the first time and every other time I jumped out the door. They didn't build puny barns when the Shedd's barn was built, in the days long before our childhoods. There were so many Shedds and brothers and neighbors leaping from this door at the same time, we were like water spilling out of the top of a rain barrel. You never knew which kid you were going to combine your molecules with down there on the ground.

The Shedd's barn was as wonderful and mysterious a place as any New Hampshire boy could hope for. Just the smell of it was enough to remind you why you were alive. And the confounding passages and corners and rooms would supply the rest of your sleepy future with those lost-in-the-endless-labyrinth dreams on which our brains and bodies keep insisting.

The Shedd's barn was connected to the main house by a cement floor passageway where they kept two or three sheep. After you slipped by the sheep, you could either turn right and go down into the cellar where homemade cider was stored in huge kegs, or you could go left into another two story structure on the back of the main house, full of every finished and unfinished project the expansive Shedd family had begun over the last twenty-five years.

The downstairs of the barn itself was a free-for-all area for the chickens and roosters, who, it seems to me, could jump out the paneless windows into the sunshine and mud that was surrounded by a rambling, well-trampled fence. Upstairs was one enormous open second story with a solid wood floor and various lengths of ropes and chains hanging from the unreachable rafters, which we, of course, somehow reached. The image of Tarzan swinging across our modest black and white TV screens was dull compared to the full-color exploits of the red-blooded boys in the rafters and on the floor.

Right next to this barn was a garage that was low enough to provide roof-leaping access to the garage and barn of the house next door. Today, the shingles and the contour and the slope of this roof are much better lodged in my memory and rank much higher in the scheme of things than whatever it was the Shedds kept inside that garage. I know there was never room to keep their VW bus in there, the bus we helped the Shedd's father fill with barrels of trash every Sunday so we could go with him to the dump.

He dropped us off at the sandpits just off the dump road, while he went to empty his trash. We practiced our flying and rolling operations with the benefit of the soft avalanches of sand to buoy our bodies launching from the cliffs that were much higher than the hay door of the Shedd's barn. We leapt and we tumbled a thousand times, and none of us knew how to measure the passing of time. We were thinking harder about something kids never call courage. Who would believe ordinary sand could smell so sweet, or earth's own grit could be so cleansing, spilling from every pocket of every kid as we climbed back into the Shedd's VW bus to head home?

The Kite

My FATHER WAS NOT ONE to do things in a halfhearted way. One cloudless afternoon of my childhood, a small bright shape blew out of the steady breeze of his conversation, another idea. He'd been wanting to do this for a long time. My father was a man-sized child, always prepared to do something to intrigue his own children. He was a doing and making kind of man. It helped that he was trained as a mechanical engineer and knew how everything worked. He also owned a sewing factory, so this latest in a measureless string of ideas was a natural. I can't say how much I think the world lost, when it lost the daily arrival of these ideas.

He had the material on hand, the cutting table and sewing machines, so why not make the biggest kite he could? We spread the fabric on the cutting table's hard brown surface that stretched the full length of the sewing factory in the upstairs of the old village store. The wooden floor creaked as your brown shoes kicked through fallen scraps of fabric while you moved along the edge of the table.

The first kite would be a trial kite, only about six feet tall, made in the traditional shape for kites, but out of a rugged blue nylon cloth. We hemmed a strong cord into the four sides, leaving an opening at each of the points, where sturdy bamboo cross-poles were hooked into the cord. The six foot kite worked beautifully, though it was a job to fly it, and it got hung up in quite a few towering trees until we added an incredible length of tail. She was a sight to see. My father was happy with the design, and a week or so later we cut and stitched the big kite.

It was well over twice my height, almost twice my father's height. It was made out of the same blue nylon. We soon realized that nothing named "string" would keep this kite tethered to the planet. My father tracked down some nylon cord that was not much thicker than string, but incredibly strong. A few thousand feet of it was wound onto a large wooden spool which was mounted on a pipe. We drove one end of the pipe into the ground. Someone held on doggedly to the upper end of the pipe, while others used the wooden handle on the spool to let the kite out or crank it in. It took at least three people to fly it. The pull would easily lift a mere human into the timeless skies.

We named the big kite "Goliath" and the little kite became "David." Flying Goliath could be dangerous business, but what exhilaration we felt when he got so high he looked like a normal puny kite. On one of our first flights, the cord actually broke, and we found the kite hours later in a tree a mile north of us. We flew Goliath in every strong wind, and spent hours with our pipe driven into the hillside of the large field that belonged to the Shedd family, behind our house. Kids from all over town came to help my father and the rest of us fly Goliath. At times we had reports of Goliath having been spotted high above the southern regions of town, although we lived in the northern part of town. David, incidentally, wound up in a treetop too high to reach, in front of a house down the road from us. He stayed there, fighting for the last shreds of his life for many years.

Like children everywhere, we used to send messages up the string of the kite, on a ripped piece of paper folded or taped around the string. But there was something very mysterious about sending a message up to the heights where Goliath climbed. It made you think twice about the message you wrote. Nothing silly was quite good enough. And it would be a very long time, if ever, before you encountered your tiny truth again close up.

Years later, when I was grown big enough to know better, another irresistible idea swirled from my father's brain. It was the middle of winter and the lake in town had frozen with a perfectly smooth surface of dazzling ice, with no snow on it. There was a high wind. My father resurrected Goliath from the barn and we took it out on the lake, taking turns holding on for dear life to the kite's crossbars as we sailed on our skates at breakneck speed across the lake, my father all the while shouting about the dynamics of tacking. There is a vision I have, that won't go away. I see it now. My father, bareheaded in the paralyzing wind, sailing a giant blue kite away from me, away from me across the soundless ice.

The Dinner Table

LARGE FAMILY GATHERINGS ROUND a dinner table, particularly on holidays, are occasions for generous celebrations. Some families celebrate while they are having dinner; some celebrate immediately afterwards. It's a case of how much you're willing to swallow together.

During my own childhood, I'm happy to report, not only the holidays but practically every dinner was a real celebration: a celebration of our eccentricities. In those days it was a tribal tradition for families to sit down and eat together. It was something you did every day and you could count on doing it. It was a lot of work, and time consuming, but in the long run saved all the expense of psychiatrists for seven people.

My father sat at one end of the huge mahogany table, my mother at the other. There was no head or tail, although my father had a chair with arms, and my mother was on the end closer to the kitchen. Years before we were born, my father had missed his calling to be an actor and a comedian, so he satisfied this urge at the dinner table. As our ringleader, he taught all of us the lessons that would stay with us for life. He taught us to be consistently impolite, to blurt out anything and everything on your mind at any moment, never to listen to anyone else at the table, to be completely silent only if you were in the middle of thinking of a malnourished and tortuous pun.

The din at the dinner table was so bad that my father put his engineering skills to work to make things run more smoothly. Everyone was talking at once; and a concurrent phenomenon manifested itself: no one was listening. If you asked for the salt and pepper, no one passed them. So my father bought seven miniature salt and pepper shakers. The son or daughter whose turn it was to set the table drummed down a pair at each place, and we never had to ask again. We also had our own separate butter dishes, with little pats on them made by a butter segmenter that sliced up a whole stick at once.

These improvements helped things along, but dinner at our house would have been completely impossible without the large Lazy Susan. When we were not eating, the Lazy Susan was often busy spinning kids on the floor, but during dinner time, it was in the middle of the table spinning mashed potatoes and gravy around and around like a record player on 78 rpm. It was a trick to get what you wanted to stop in front of you, without causing a dangerous pileup.

And so we ate bountifully, and the small talk was momentous, though, as I said, no one was ever listening. Occasionally several people actually got into the same conversation at the same moment in time. When we did, it ran something like this:

A brother: I have a wicked canker in my mouth.

My father: A what?

Me: Don't answer him!

My father: You've got a *what?*

My brother: I've got a canker.

My father: You're welcome.

My mother's favorite expression at the table was "May I get a word in edgewise?" We all got a kick out of that and took to mimicking it. It really did describe our predicament. There never was a conversation with so many "edgewise" words crammed into it.

My mother managed all through our childhoods to produce meals. Some of them were good. But you could never exactly say that her heart was in it. Everyone admired her memory and her concentration. She could regale you with details of the lives of far distant relatives dead for two generations, but more often than not, she could not remember to turn on the stove at the opportune moment when there was something there to cook, or to turn the stove off to take advantage of that propitious moment when the food was done.

We didn't go unnourished, but our nourishment had more to do with the quirks in our personalities and sudden meteors of insight flashing from the chaos. The source of much insight was a sense of humor that had been passed down to my father through several generations, and the source of much of the humor was my mother's unending tilts against the kitchen. But more of that the next time we sit down together...

Tilting Against the Kitchen

Not infrequently, we all sat down to dinner only to hear cries of exasperation from the kitchen: "Would you believe it? I never turned this goulash on!" We seven waited patiently while the goulash "baked." In five or ten minutes, my mother put the huge casserole dish on the table and we ate up. Your serving was warm, lukewarm or ice-cold, depending on how near the edge or the center of the dish it came from.

More frequently, my mother forgot to turn the oven or the burners off and call us to dinner. She had become involved in something like reading a newspaper. We came to expect as a matter of course, that almost once a week the kitchen would fill with dense, choking fumes, that got no notice until they started to unfurl into the rest of the house. You couldn't breathe these fumes without slicing your insides, so someone had to suck in a big breath and plunge through the kitchen to open the doors and windows. Over the years, a permanent black ring of smoke was painstakingly painted onto the white ceiling, radiating from a point just above the stove.

All this, naturally, was just one more ideal problem for my father to apply his engineering skills to. After several false starts, he finally installed an enormous whole-house fan in the attic of the house. When the smoke came we simply latched open all the doors from the upstairs down to the kitchen (there was a hook and eye in each doorway) and then waited it out in a smoke-free sector, until the air cleared.

Needless to say, my mother's episodes of tilting against the kitchen became the subject of many stories told in our family. One summer day, my brother Ted and I were busy playing outside when our noses simultaneously hooked a suspicious dark thread in the air, which seemed to come from the direction of the house.

Fearing the worst, we sprinted home, found it full of smoke, turned the oven off, then pulled out a large broiler tray with the most pitiful crematory remains on it we'd ever seen. What we later learned had once been a roast beef big enough to feed seven was now nothing but a flimsy charcoal shell about 4 inches long and 2 inches high that crumbled like a puffball as soon as you touched it. It was surrounded by numerous little piles of charcoal that had been potatoes in a former life.

She had achieved her major opus. She had put the roast beef in the oven in the morning, turned the oven up high and then abandoned the house for the entire day, immensely enjoying her opportunity to visit all the neighbors. When we found her, we informed her as diplomatically as possible that the dinner had become a shell of its former self, but we tried not to get too carried away. We didn't want her to get paranoid.

Year after year, through the smoke and the raw meat, the din of confused conversation, the seven pairs of salt and pepper shakers, the sad and the happy puns, and everywhere the "edgewise" words, somehow we managed to get through thousands and thousands of dinners at the Hall house. Perhaps we missed some valuable training in being civilized and well-mannered. We ate well, though. In spite of all the setbacks relative, as they say, to quality, we did very well relative to quantity. Occasionally everything came together perfectly. For special occasions my mother could cook a beautiful meal. We didn't go hungry.

But what was nourished most was something intangible about ourselves, something to do with our sense of humor, and our ability to laugh at ourselves. There was one thing my father used to say quite often at the table that I *did* hear, that got all the way through to me. He said you can lose everything else, but don't ever lose your sense of humor. It's the one thing you will really need. A simple thing to say. Almost small talk. But I don't know if I've heard anything wiser yet.

Humor got harder for all of us to hold onto. None of us knew what was coming, what, or who, was going. But humor stayed. Some proof that year after year at the big dining room table, my mother and father fed us very well.

Carnival

IN THOSE DISTANT DAYS, BEFORE the first skier pulled on the first pair of buckle boots or stepped down smugly into safety bindings, the people of Brookline participated year after year in the town's most important winter ritual: the three day PTA Winter Carnival. As usual, my father was one of the principals, getting the ribbons printed, testing out his stopwatch, fretting over the ropes and tires in the obstacle course. But every other father and mother of every kid I knew was there too. What else would you do on the cold days in the middle of winter when everyone else was out skiing and skating? Stay home and watch the snowy television set?

Saturday was often a day of skating. On Saturday night, tired skaters sat on unfolded chairs or danced on the hard floor at the Carnival Ball, while the Carnival King and Queen sat on their thrones. On Sunday, the contest moved from Lake Potanipo down Route 13 to the Brookline Ski Tow on Muscatanipus Hill. The mountain had an active ski area back then, operated by one DeRossa, who came from someplace in Massachusetts, where, of course, all shady operators came from. In earlier days, when it was owned by Brookliners, you could ski for free if you helped pack the hill by sidestepping up it with a team of other skiers.

The hill had a rope tow that was likely the most dangerous rope tow anywhere in the world. The heavy, splinterpacked rope slithered up in its own gorge. When you tried to pick it up it bent your frail body right over and your knuckles dragged over the snow and ice and rocks. Sometimes, especially on cold days, it clung to your mittens or scarf or jacket. One time an older brother had to shed half his wardrobe to keep from getting dragged into the giant wheel at the top. The emergency trip bar was skied through hourly by kids who couldn't get off, and more than half the time it didn't stop anything. Wool mittens spun around the wheel and headed back down the hill. No one was killed on this lift, but there were numerous injuries over the years.

On carnival day, the hill was set up with a slalom course on one slope and a downhill course on another. One year I proved to all my Brookline friends that I wasn't a wimp. The downhill course was set up on the steep slope, with only a few gates and the conditions were fast. It looked a little treacherous, and most of the downhillers carefully took a few extra passes across the hill to avoid going too fast. My brother Ted and I were used to speed from our nonstop skiing up north, and we both took it straight, even pumping up more speed at the starting gate. The other kids were astonished we had the "guts" to do that. Of course we won first place in our respective age groups. That felt good.

Another event was the skiing obstacle course, set up at the ball park, probably a little more fun for the inventors than for the skiers. After all the events, the ribbons were awarded. A boy's and girl's grand trophy was given to the overall winners, and they got to keep these at home over the fireplace until the next year's carnival. Sometimes there were basketball games, the married men versus the single men and the married women versus the single women, or ski movies were shown. Other happenings were spawned out of various imaginations and organizations in town.

I vividly remember the skating events on the lake. Perhaps that's because I was no skater, but participated anyway. We had hot cocoa and huge bonfires, burning everything in sight. There was usually a large circle cleared for the speed race, and one year my father put down his stopwatch and picked up his old black-box movie camera to record my laps around this course, not skating, but running strictly on the sides of my ankles in old beat-up brown-leather hockey skates, a half a lap and then more than a lap behind the rest of the pack of boys. How I lost. But how we all enjoyed the hundreds of laps it became over the years, watching home movies on cold winter nights, before we staggered up to bed exhausted.

Dancing

Some of our sturdy religious New England forebears (who left our little towns the good looks they have today) could tell you everything you ever wanted to know about *sects*, but very little about homophones. That is why some towns had not one Protestant church, but two or more white glittering temples, lifting the village above the forest and giving the people their social and architectural focus.

My father and mother moved to this town about the time when I must have been something more than a twinkle in my father's eye, about two thousand three hundred and forty church services ago. When they first arrived they were interested in the social life of the two churches that stood on Main Street about as far apart as you could scale a contribution plate. My mother attended a service at the Congregational church where only six other souls were saved with hers, and then she went to the Methodist church where twenty-five citizens politely sat listening to a fire-and-brimstone and over-the-hill pastor.

She decided to do something about this. After a great meeting of the minds, and a hugely successful oyster stew dinner (cooked by one Carl Clifford, the town's only patriot) that was served with coffee that was brewed in a clean diaper in water that never came to a boil over the church's kitchen wood stove, people put aside their differences and decided to join the two churches into one. One church became the Church of Christ and the other became the town's Youth Center, a building that served Brookline's youthful needs for decades.

Recently the inside of this old church was renovated into a gorgeous library and the outside restored to its own remarkable luster, its lusty New England voice ringing out clearly again to the world and to the passerby. Fortunately the people who inhabit our town today are still wise enough to forego plastic golden arches and stick with the white wooden arches some carpenter devised long ago. It proves you can all believe in God together and still keep your individual character, but you can't do the same thing with fast food.

Getting back to the real topic, *sects*, there never was much difference between the theology or the philosophy of the two churches. The chief difference was that the Congregational church had a squat, square steeple with short rails and corner finials pointing toward the skies, and huge black clocks on three sides of the belfry. Even today this church looks solid, grounded to the earth. The Methodist church, on the other hand, the current library, has a tall slender tower and a thin spire that reaches high up to pierce the sunrises and the sunsets. It is ethereal. The weather vane at the very top lives in a different weather than we do down below.

When I was a boy, old enough to sing in the junior choir and carry the contribution plate to the wooden ends of the rows of pews, I got signed up to go to Arthur Murray dance lessons in the ethereal church, which was the youth center at that time. Boys with their scarce hair touched up with tonic and combed neatly, and girls wearing dresses and freckles fox-trotted around the gym floor of the big echoing room where the brimstone sermons had once been preached.

We were led by a tall, very clean-cut man whom I always fancied to be Arthur Murray *himself*, as we kicked through the occasional islands of green cleaning dust left behind by the woman who was janitor to the town, who swept the floor with a wide push broom just before we started. I remember these dances not because I ever learned to dance, but because it was the only time I got to get close to a girl named Desiré Rumore, who was beautiful, and whose first name and last name smacked of everything good and bad in a small town.

Desiré Rumore! We waltzed and we pushed and we twirled, and we never dropped the red balloon Mr. Murray stuck between us. We never popped it either. Some balloon! There are many things you can do without. You can do without a lot of hamburgers. But you can never do without steeples, or red balloons.

The Courage of It

WHEN YOU DRIVE YOUR CAR through the center of our little town on your way to the hardware store in the next town to buy a new can of flux and an extra propane gas cylinder to resweat your frozen, burst pipes underneath your house in the middle of winter, you first pass between the yellow town hall and a white church and then you negotiate a very sharp bend in the road, where you either borrow a bit of the sidewalk if there is no schoolchild walking there or borrow a bit of the other lane if there is no oncoming truck, or else you grip the wheel tightly because you can't see either thing coming anyway. I've grown to love this corner. I love the pre-bulldozer logic of it. I love the courage of it. If it ever gets straightened out, I'll begin to think about moving to Maine.

Just as you weather this turn you see on your right an unassuming vacant lot with a curious empty building at the back of it. An out-of-town owner refaced the outside one year with cedar shingles, but only finished staining part of them dark brown. That was so long ago that the unstained ones are halfway there to matching the others. This little building was once our schoolhouse and the unassuming lot was the playground for the first, second and third grades. In very early times, when the road-builders' children were going to school, the building had a better personality with the help of a handsome cupola on top.

Depending on how quickly you take the corner, this two-room school with its tiny dirt yard seems either very quaint or very pathetic by today's standards, but our teachers, our grand imaginations and, above all, an unending supply of sunshine and fresh air, made it room enough for us. We were engaged in the remarkably serious business of having a childhood. We had a shoulder-top computer at every desk with that fastest of processing chips, a child's brain, and we had a gymnasium the size of the whole outdoors.

We were country boys and girls and pre-Socratic philosophers. Our first encounter with Aristotle was one Mrs. Shea. She wasn't simply the first grade teacher. She was an angel, with a pair of pliers in her desk for pulling teeth. Even the tooth-pulling only *looked* brutal. In reality, everything about Mrs. Shea was gentle, and you couldn't have had a kinder person to make you take the first crunch of that peculiar, tart apple you'd heard stories about in Sunday School.

I don't remember much about her classroom. I remember it had a green "blackboard." Here was a pretty nifty word lesson right away on the first day of school. Why the heck didn't she call it the "greenboard"? I remember the beautifully executed alphabet across the front of the room. I remember something called "phonetics," which I'm not sorry I learned, and I remember an alternate method she had of pulling teeth, one that was used on me one time.

I was told to stand about fifteen paces from the white door that opened into the classroom near the corner next to a big sink where older brothers had warned me about kids getting their mouths washed out with soap. That must have been before Mrs. Shea. She directed a boy to tie one end of a string around my tooth while a girl tied the other end to the tarnished brass doorknob. I was instructed to plant my feet firmly. I don't remember if I was blindfolded. This may not have been a wholly new form of capital punishment, but it was new to me.

A crowd of my peers gathered around me to witness this martyrdom, and yet another girl was chosen to slam the door at the teacher's command. I was certain it would end in tears and disgrace. I heard the numb directive from Mrs. Shea echo through my skull and in that same moment I was surprised to learn my tooth was already out. I had felt almost nothing. I gained the adulation of the gawking, wheedling crowd. Mrs. Shea wrapped the tooth in a tissue and I grabbed it and put it securely into the prison of my pocket, very glad to have turned another of life's niggling corners. I looked at my admirers. "That musta hert *sumpin wickit*," they said. "Naw. Not *too* bad," I said.

Scratching Dirt

OUR TWO-ROOM YELLOW SCHOOLHOUSE held something else in store for us once we got beyond those ethereal tooth-losing years under the guidance of Mrs. Shea. Our third grade teacher was as big a disaster as Mrs. Shea was a success. Her name was Mrs. Madrone, so, naturally, we called her Mrs. Trombone.

She was large and histrionic. Every day she wore a blue gauzy dress with small white dots and perspiration all over it. My older brother alerted me that she was apt to throw fits when she was at a loss for what to do. Without warning, she'd scream at the class and sweep everything off her desk with the loose back of her arm, while we trembled like puppies behind our wee wooden desks. Papers, pencils, pens, books and everything flew into the air before our eyes and swooped to the floor. This was the year we studied behavioral psychology.

Inside that schoolroom our childhood was being put to sleep like a stray dog. But somehow the hours passed and in no time we were bobbing about the playground again. Looking back today, I feel sure we spent more time outside than inside. We were small-town kids. We had our priorities straight. Outdoor education was far more important than indoor education. We traveled very far in the schoolyard. We played out all the immemorial battles and fantasies of childhood on the small dirt rectangle of the playground.

Running out the door and down the three stone steps into the sunshine, there was generally a chorus of frantic voices: NO DROPSIES, NO KICKSIES, NO BOOTSIES, NO PUSHIES, NO SHOVESIES, NO MOVESIES, and on and on, as we fumbled in our pockets for our hard-won assortments of marbles. Every day something got added to this Draconian code of marbles, and it got harder and harder to think of stuff you *could* do.

We spent timeless hours in the vertical and horizontal cabals of those rainbow-colored crystal balls. My brother Ted had what I thought must be the biggest marble collection in the whole town, hundreds of them he kept in a white tin box at home, big ones and small ones, clear and solid and whorled. I don't know if it was a tribute to his skill, or just his hoarding instincts, but I was respectful and amazed. Marbles are as magic and magnanimous as childhood. I can't think of any better preparation for life than playing marbles, or a better grounding in some basics of social behavior, politics, aesthetics and physics.

Other games we played were limited only by our imaginations and our imaginations were not limited at all. For several years, David McNabb and I had the same routine. In a corner against the fence and near the road, a hospital with many rooms and hallways and doors was scratched carefully into the dirt by the well-scuffed toes of our brown shoes. These imaginary walls were almost real, and so were the imaginary nurses. Once the walls were up, the work began:

"Doctor Hall, come right away on the double please. A man with a broken leg just walked into room 6."

"Be right there, Doctor McNabb. Have a nurse throw him on the bed. Don't take any chances. It could be serious. We might need to call in Dr. Shedd."

Dr. Shedd was a very busy man, but he could usually be brought in for emergencies, even when he was in the middle of marbles. Dr. McNabb and I both knew that his grandfather was famous in the north country for setting broken bones in skiers. He was solid.

One time on the playground when Dr. McNabb was just being an ordinary kid for a while, he taught me a new way to tie my shoe laces. Make two loops and tie them together! I was flabbergasted. It was far simpler and more efficient than the way I had learned from my parents. I couldn't believe a mere kid could have this kind of knowledge. I had to rethink my whole world. In less than a minute he had unlaced my mind and made me take a giant step. There was no one to say if it was a forward or a backward step. But I took it.

Trout Tank

SOME SCIENTIFIC EXPERIMENTS SAY MORE about the people performing them than they do about the world they are supposed to illuminate. This was likely to be the case when my father proposed a project to my brother Ted for his seventh grade science fair. But we never dismissed my father's ideas quickly, because we knew they could lead just about anywhere.

They sketched on graph paper, transmuted lines into numbers, and drove off to buy the plywood. They ripped the pieces, screwed them together and put it on legs. They built compartments into it, and made tiny doors that could slide in and out. They sanded thoroughly, caulked it so no water could escape, and painted everything forest green. Ingenious. Dozens of possibilities would be available to the amazed trout, depending, of course, on how the doors were placed.

I went with them to a local fire hole to do some very demanding fishing. The trout had to be virtually the same size, healthy, old enough to think straight, and hooked so as not to hurt them. At last, we had four speckled trout in a pail and took them home to the larger pails which would become their home for the next few weeks.

Ted spent long scientific hours with his trout. At first, he made the simplest of mazes. He kept meticulous records in the pre-ruled pages of a notebook. He used my father's stopwatch to time them from the opening of the starting gate to the gobbling of the reward. He set down other observations too. The trout had names: Arthur, Fred, Frank, and Lucy.

It wasn't easy getting these guys into the tank or out again. A lot of water got splashed. Worse, the trout didn't seem to be *learning* anything. As soon as Ted made up a maze that was even slightly puzzling, they were at a dead loss. They either scooted around banging into the walls or they hovered in one spot doing nothing. But Ted was persistent and my father helpful.

After one week, it seemed the trout were making headway. Once, Frank zipped right through a Byzantine maze. But Ted tried and tried and could never get him to do it again. We began to suspect the whole thing was entirely hit or miss, but Ted maintained his results showed slow progress. Frank, at least, seemed promising.

Ted's trout became his pals. In spite of the disappointing graphs and statistics, and the hard work, he thoroughly enjoyed the whole thing, and my father kept him going. To be honest, the experiment was an abysmal failure. On the other hand, we all came to have a certain respect for these trout. We hoped, I think, that their spirits would never be broken by the ugly human hand of science reaching down into their private element; that they would go on doing just what they wanted to do forever. We were secretly very proud of them.

On the morning of the science fair, my father and Ted transported the tank to the junior high gymnasium, filled it with water and hung enormous signs and dense statistics about. The public was impressed. Frank, Arthur, Fred and Lucy shuffled comfortably round their pails, and the six of them waited for the judges to come by.

Ted made the most complicated maze the tank could handle. That way he could not only show off the sophistication of his equipment, but, at the end, he would have a way to explain the trouts' failure. He put Frank in the starting gate, and punched the stopwatch as he slid open the door. With three serious judges watching, along with my father and a number of other spectators, Frank leapt through the gate and whirled through the entire maze in ten seconds flat, without a single hesitation. Ted won first prize at the science fair.

The next day I went with Ted and my father to the fire hole. We laughed as we said good-bye to the four fish, one at a time. Frank was last. Was it a gush of imagination, or did I detect the water-clouded image of a sly wink as I looked down into the unsettled pail at Frank's face? No, I quickly put the thought out of mind, but my father did give a little wink at Ted and me, as he picked up the pail and handed it to Ted, who poured Frank home.

Scooters and Skateboards

THANK HEAVEN FOR THOSE THINGS that stop you dead in your tracks, and then let you live to tell the story. My father was very good at finding those things. One year, when I was still getting used to having a second digit hitched to my age, my father became aware of a new sport called skateboarding, in its infancy at that time.

True to his fashion, he could not be satisfied with anything but a top-of-the-line model. After a lot of research, he found one he liked. Made of laminated oak, with a long slender shape and graceful nose and tail, and heavy wheels, this skateboard was a pleasure to look at. But he still wasn't happy. He fixed bigger wheels on it, and better axles and bearings, and put two extra coats of varnish on the wood. When he was done, it was the Cadillac of skateboards.

Our bright white farmhouse with glossy black shutters stood in the sunshine at the bottom of a gently rising road. You'd have to hike quite a few miles up this road before you reached the highpoint. It was perfect for skateboarding, at least if you didn't turn the sharp corner just past our house and go down the very steep hill to the store (where, during the winter, we used to play chicken on our metal runner sleds with the dangerous Shedd family).

About this time, my oldest brother came back from Europe with a little red Vespa scooter. We kids practiced buzzing this cute machine up and down our road. Back then it could take hours before a car would come to pop your milkweed pod, and kids, skateboards, bicycles, pogo-sticks and Vespa scooters had little competition from cars for use of the road.

Of course it didn't take long to figure out that this Vespa and this skateboard went together. My brother Ted and I hummed up Old Milford Road as far as Sonny Farwell's house, one of us riding on the back hanging onto the skateboard. The scooter had a treacherous habit of suddenly freezing up and going into a skid, so we weren't allowed to drive over 25 miles an hour on it, helmeted and tense all the way. The skateboard gave you much more of the genuine wind-in-your-hair, freedom-of-the-open-road feeling as you downhilled all the way to our house.

Ted was the only person I knew who dared to take the corner and go past the Shedd's house to the store. It was a perilous speed you'd pick up on Steam Mill Hill; frankly, thoroughly foolish to even think of it. But that didn't stop Ted. I stood and watched many times, in fear, not taking a breath until he finally jumped off where the road leveled out.

One time I watched Ted on this steep finish to nearly a three mile run he had managed gracefully. But I had a bad feeling, and, sure enough, disaster struck. The skateboard hit a small pebble in the road and stopped dead. Ted, of course, kept going at the same planetary speed he'd been going. I never saw anyone's legs move so fast trying to catch up to a person's shoulders and head, which (in accord with one of those laws of physics you can't break even if you dare to) were way out in the lead. Ted made a plucky effort to catch up to himself, and didn't make it; but at least he had the luck to be heading toward the tall grass on the side of the road, where he crashed.

He came out of it pretty thoroughly bruised, I hoped to God humbled as well, but I'm not sure of that. The skateboard came through without even a scratch on her hull. We hung her up in the barn next to where we parked the Vespa scooter, and they both started dreaming of the open road, and fighting the dust.

One year that scooter disappeared somewhere. But the skateboard stayed for three decades until my nine-year old son found it, was convinced on the spot, and brought it to our house. He left it out in the rain twice, so I had to put a slender bolt through, pull the laminations back together, and paint two more coats of varnish on it. Then I made a better place to hang it in the garage.

The Stonehouse Brook

"DON'T TAKE US FOR *granite!*" This pun has probably occurred at one time or another to every child who has grown up in the granite state, and to every political pundit observing the New Hampshire presidential primary season. It crops up as often as the rocks themselves do.

It certainly occurred to us during the many hours we played in and around and under a remarkable glacial pile of boulders known as the Stonehouse, a local landmark with an equally interesting natural and human history, a destination just far enough through the woods from our house to make it unattractive to most adults. This is the place where we survived our childhoods by the skin of our teeth, and the grown-ups never knew the tests we passed.

There is something *granitous* that grows in the New Hampshire soul, something as hard as stone but as soft as sculpture. Our granite is the light gray granite, darkened by the weather and greened by lichen. Our stone is everywhere. Trees root themselves in it; brooks skid under it; squirrels sprint over it. To be a citizen of New Hampshire you have to build a stone wall. The walls shadow our roads and run like blood vessels through our woods. The rocks bubble up to the surface of our fields and garden patches, where we skim them off into piles.

We've made the rocks our own. We've brought them over to our side, even if we sometimes take them for granite ourselves. As another shameless pundit might like to have punned it: we've taken a *lichen* to them. Our oldest stone walls are more useful today than they were to the original builders. They serve our collective memory, and they help determine our personalities.

No wonder the kids who grew up with the Stonehouse nearby developed interesting personalities. With no grown-ups to keep us in check we were lucky a few of us didn't *lose* our personalities. As usual, it was those Shedds who thought up the challenges.

The rocks and cliffs around the Stonehouse were high enough for my brothers many years later to practice rock climbing when they were taking ROTC in college. But we didn't take any ropes with us when we were kids. That would have been too high-tech. We were busy with Fox and Geese, or Cowboys and Indians, or Cops and Robbers or any other variation on good guys and bad guys that would get you hanging off the side of a cliff, risking your life for the cause of good or of evil.

"*I got you!*" a kid shouted, somehow giving equal emphasis to the "got" and the "you." If you were balanced on a cliff, and an Indian put an arrow through your shoulder, you had to dive convincingly off the edge, bounce off a sloping ledge ten feet below and tumble to the bottom of the rocks, or roll by chance into a grotto where you could come to life again after you died for a minute, and then reciprocate. You had to be a good actor. Halfhearted screams or groans wouldn't do.

These deaths might involve vertical drops of quite a few times the length of your little body. It is probably not a good idea even today, thirty years later, to reveal to grown-ups all the things we did on those rocks. As far as we were concerned, those rocks were dragged in there by the glacial drift for only one purpose, to test us. If we couldn't pass this test, no other test would count.

We all knew the real enemy was the rock itself. But over the years with the help of many dangers and adventures, we brought those rocks over to our side. Eventually, we really took a *lichen* to them. Below the cliffs and ledges of the granite deposit, a small brook, the "Stonehouse Brook," barely bigger than a rivulet, runs through a defile and along the draw until it comes to a larger brook that goes into a river that flows across an invisible borderline into another state.

You can sit on a light gray rock in the middle of this brook in the cold fall air and look down at the fine-veined, yellow, and orange and blood-red leaves floating happily in the water. You can think about *leaves*, but the rocks and the crags of the Stonehouse rising above you will be changing you, even if you don't want them to. They will be drifting secretly into your bones.

Barnacle Bill the Sailor

IMAGINE THE TOWN I GREW up in. There were over eight hundred people in it and only one was a cross-dresser; and that was my father. As with the other pranks he played on the town hall stage, the rehearsals at home went on for weeks before the show. The timing had to be perfect. Music and singing filled our house.

Imagine our New England town hall, with the large upstairs room that held a full-size stage and decorated set, where the selectmen and the moderator sat behind a table at town meeting, and where generations of amateur actors strutted their stuff before unbelieving audiences.

My mother and I entered and sat in one of the double wooden folding chairs set up end to end with all the others. The room was filling rapidly. I ran a finger along the chair to make the wooden slats rattle. The large curtain painted with woodland scenes loomed in front of us. "Oh the roar of the greasepaint, the smell of the crowd," I said to my mother, trying out one of my father's typical inversions.

Later I learned that my father's little skit had been the highlight of the evening's entertainment and it lived on in townfolk's memories for quite a few years. I also learned that a few people had been scandalized. They weren't accustomed to seeing men in drag or boys carrying whiskey bottles in our little town.

My brother Tom sat on the edge of the stage and played a couple of introductory chords on his guitar. The curtain went up and there my father sat in a rocking chair with a floor lamp on one side of him and a door standing all alone on the other side of him. He wore a tight red dress, with nylons, high heels and a beautiful blond wig. His cheeks were pink and his lips bright red. His character was very well developed, with the help of two grapefruit held in place somehow under the dress. He was a vision of beauty.

My brother Ted, wearing a sailor suit and hat, swaggered out from offstage and banged roughly on the door. His face was begrimed and he swung a bottle of Seagrams Seven whiskey in his hand. My father's sweet falsetto voice rang out through the hall: *Who's that knocking on my door? Who's that knocking on my door? cried the fair young maiden.*

Ted caroled back in the lowest and huskiest voice he could produce, though it hadn't been long since his real voice had changed: *It's me, myself and nobody else, cried Barnacle Bill the sailor.* Then he belched rudely to the back rows.

He took a swig of whiskey and reeled. The gorgeous falsetto voice sang back to him and the rough sailor voice barked back at *her* as they went on and on through all the verses: *Won't you tell me where you've been? cried the fair young maiden.*

I'm back from sailing over the sea. I'm all lit up like a Christmas tree, cried Barnacle Bill the sailor.

I'll come down and let you in, cried the fair young maiden.

Let's hear your feet upon the floor. Hurry before I break the door, cried Barnacle Bill the sailor.

If you're drunk you must stay out, cried the fair young maiden.

Oh whiskey is the life of man. I drink it from an old tin can, cried Barnacle Bill the sailor.

I looked around the hall. Most of the audience was lit up with laughter, but a few looked worried, certain older women in particular. I heard someone whisper, "I hope he's wearing *underwear* under that dress!" There were many more verses before they finally came to the end: *Lips that drink will not touch mine, cried the fair young maiden.*

Kissin's not what I have in mind. Now open the door, and draw the blind, cried Barnacle Bill the sailor.

The curtain banged down. The audience whistled and applauded. The curtain came up again and Ted was sitting in my father's lap with his arms around his neck. The curtain rolled down slowly and up again slowly. My father and my brother stood bowing side by side, my father with a grapefruit in each hand. The curtain went down again with a thud.

The Big Baloney

ONE DELIGHTFUL, BREEZY SUMMER day in 1961, I sat alone at our dining room table in my white T-shirt, rolled up dungarees and black sneakers, my butched head almost as bare as my arms, and I looked down at the sandwich my mother had brought me for lunch, a slice of pale baloney stained with yellow mustard, and a piece of flat processed cheese between two die-cut rectangles of bread as white as sugar, on a plate designed to withstand a blow against the concrete wall of an air raid shelter. All this was considered completely normal for a ten year old boy in those days. In fact, I loved baloney sandwiches, and I dove in greedily.

Little did I know that, in the next few months, I would undergo a luncheon meat crisis that would put me twenty years ahead of the rest of America. We were into the sixties. The news was full of John Kennedy and the Bay of Pigs. It would be a decade of staggering turmoil and upheaval.

My father's stitching business was located in the upstairs of the building that held the town's Red & White grocery store. We had our own access to the store by the back stairs, both day and night. So my father passed by a cardboard box many times a week, where he deposited our name on a slip of paper to enter a sales promotion contest to win a giant baloney. He dreamed of keeping a family of seven supplied with their baloney needs indefinitely.

Naturally, we won this thing. Jubilantly, we drove down to the store to retrieve it. A photographer from the *Brookline News* was there to take a picture of two of my brothers, my sister and myself standing in front of the store holding this sixty-five pound baloney that was strapped to a board and spanned the length of the four of us standing side by side. It was not just long. It had the diameter of a 78 rpm record.

We lashed it onto the top of the car and took it home and hauled it onto the dining room table. Immediately we engaged in a reevaluation of our high spirits. It would have been easier to cope with a telephone pole blown down in a hurricane and left lying across our dining room table than to figure out how we were going to use this meat without wasting it.

My father ticked off some marks and cut off equal segments for our friends and company employees. These were wrapped separately and carried by car to various locations around town. But we were still left with a mammoth amount of sandwich meat, and there was nothing to do but start contriving our diet around it.

The first week we ate baloney every day from about 10 o'clock on. (I don't remember that we ever stooped to having it for breakfast.) I indulged in my loyalty to baloney before, during and after school and every night. It was a baloney paradise for me. I couldn't get enough. I didn't care how many animals of what species it took to make it, and I didn't worry that just one piece rolled up with mustard was really enough to make a meal in itself. I'd eat two or three pieces at a time.

After more than a week of this, I was sitting again at the table, biting into a baloney and cheese sandwich when a certain indefinable and unearthly nausea arrived like a stray dog to roam among my taste buds. I felt this nausea spread like a bad rumor into the lobes of my brain, and then flee from there, like a criminal, into the protection of my stomach and intestines. My hair stood on end as the revulsion passed over my whole body.

That was the end. I could not touch another piece of baloney for about twenty years, and even today I have trouble thinking of eating that stuff, though now my kids are dabbling in it, partly, I think, as a form of protest against my irrational prejudice. But I'm a child of the sixties. I came of age with the help of a six foot long promotional baloney and learned the hard way that you really *can* get too much of a bad idea.

I also know I'd never have learned if I hadn't loved it so much. And now I've told you everything I know about luncheon meat.

Pull Candy

THE WORLD IS DIVIDED into just two kinds of people: the ones who stretch you and the ones who shrink you. I know this from a little hunched woman whom I outstripped in height when I was about 12 years old, who was something like my step great-grandmother and who invited me down to her house on a Saturday afternoon in the middle of my childhood to make pull candy.

I yanked on a pair of tongue-tied shoes and rambled down our dirt driveway, around a stone wall, past some rose bushes and white lilacs to her house. This was a journey of about 100 feet in space, and about 100 years in time.

Gram Perin opened the white door for me when I knocked, and I entered the tiny house that was as cozy as a rabbit warren. The couch in the middle of the room was occupied, as usual, by a line of dolls and stuffed animals out of Mother Goose. They looked as comfortable and as cordial as ever. I had never known them to lose their composure. I went and sat with them.

> *Old woman, old woman, old woman, said I!*
> *Whither, ah whither, ah whither so high?*
> *To sweep the cobwebs from the sky,*
> *And I'll be with you by and by.*

Gram's voice croaked the verse as familiar to me as an old hymn, as she held up one of the dolls. There had been some confusion in my mind when I was much younger, whether *she* was perhaps Mother Goose herself. At any rate, she measured into me the sounds and the rhythms of language and of life and death as deftly as Mother Goose would have if she were alive.

Another time when I had come to make pull candy, Gram had said the queerest thing as I stood on her front door-stoop about to leave. "You are going to be a writer when you grow up," she announced softly. What a thing to say to a twelve year old boy. I laughed at her for at least ten years. On the same occasion, after she noticed me thinking about how much taller than her I was already, she said to me, "I used to be much taller than this, but Mrs. Butterfield shrank me." Mrs. Butterfield was the woman who came in to look after Gram occasionally. Gram was pulling toward a hundred years, after all.

Her husband had been a very well known minister and the author of a number of books, one of them the story of how he cured himself of paralysis by faith healing. Gram collected anthologies of his sermons along with quotations for daily consumption. Her books were called, *The Optimist's Good Morning, The Optimist's Good Night, The Optimist Day by Day* and so on. These Unitarian Universalists were unusual people. They were deeply religious, but tolerant and liberal at the same time, a rare combination.

When George Landor Perin died, he and Gram had spent their lives and fortunes on good works. She was in her eighties and there was nothing left for her to live on. So she started a business, a gift shop and mail order enterprise that supported her through her nineties. She radiated such warmth and generosity that everything and everyone she came near turned to gold.

Gram announced that the candy was up to temperature. We huddled by the counter in her tiny warm kitchen while she laid the tall thermometer gently on a tea towel and let the candy begin to cool. We stood with our heads at the same level, waiting, and finally pulling the warm, butter-scotch colored goo into long bands before she cut them off into pieces with a sharp knife.

It was spring and the rain and the coolness were making me grow taller. But the warmth was shrinking her. So we came to be the same height. My fingers were growing deft, and could sweep the cobwebs from the sky in her kitchen. Still, she was much better than me at pulling candy. "Like this," she said, and demonstrated with her ancient, spotted, knobby fingers. "Like this. Like this."

The Big Earth

THERE'S A SQUARE THAT ALMOST resembles a city block in the middle of this little town, formed when four roads were drawn in the landscape and houses and churches gathered along the lines. At one time the lines must have been brown and easily erased, but they were redrawn in black ink later on, and seem to be there to stay.

In an era when there was no question about them knowing every animal and human soul that lived in every house on this square, two boys stood in a field of tall grass in the middle of the houses, in the very bull's eye of the town. One boy was big-eared and sandy-haired, and wore a white T-shirt, dungarees and sneakers. The other boy was brown-haired and freckle-faced and wore a white T-shirt and dungarees and moccasins. The big-eared one was me. The other was my best friend, David Shedd.

The sky was much bluer and the sun brighter that day than usual. This phenomenon was observed all over New England, and was caused by the fact that schools had just let out for the summer all over New England. There were only a few white wisps of clouds straight above the two boys' heads.

David was pointing an arrow into the sky. It had been only an hour's work to find a good birch sapling and carve it into a bow and make a couple of straight and deadly arrows, and now we were trying them out. David aimed at 90 degrees to the surface of the earth and pulled the taut string back until the tip of the arrow was just clear of the nocking point. He held on with all his strength, then tipped everything about two degrees in the direction of the church, and let go.

The arrow flew out of sight. *I shot an arrow in the air; it came to earth I know not where,* the big-eared one recited, and barely finished as the arrow buzzed into view and stung the ground about twelve feet from where we were standing.

I strung up the other arrow while David fetched the first. I pointed at the wispy clouds straight above, pulled back with all my strength, held my breath as I tipped it one degree towards the Shedd's house, then let go. *I shot an arrow in the air; it didn't come down, but I don't care,* sang David, as my arrow shot out of sight and then came back to me like a boomerang, landing less than six feet away.

Without knowing it, we were demonstrating what airplane pilots like to call the "big sky" theory, except this was the "big earth" theory. We were sure there was plenty of space on earth for an arrow to land without killing one of two inconspicuous boys standing on the earth's green surface.

David re-nocked his arrow and pointed at the same wispy clouds. He let fly. *I shot an arrow in the air; and now it's sticking in my hair,* I improvised, as David suddenly crouched to the ground with both arms over his head, and the arrow stung the green earth again halfway between David and me.

Since I have lived to tell you this story, you know that the "big earth" theory has some merit, and though I haven't seen David for many years, I know that he is still alive and has stories to tell to his own children. For those of you who are parents and are reading this story out loud to children who have bows and arrows, I will leave a little white space here for you to fill with rationalizations and disclaimers and windy explanations as quickly as you can.

{   }

For my part I have no explanation, unless there were some angels that flew above our childhoods, perhaps those wispy clouds. Perhaps they caught the arrows when they climbed out of our sight and threw them down just far enough from where we stood to save us.

Maybe there is something weighty to say about this, looking back. I could say that we aimed high and dangerously, but we never harmed a living thing. I could say we never took aim at churches or houses. I could say death stings too quickly, but the earth is greener and broader than it seems. I could say other things. But the truth is I really don't know *what* to say about it.

The News

Back when it took only three digits to tell the town's population, and you always knew who the last digit was and who was responsible for adding it; back when the most heinous crime in the schools was sticking chewing gum on the bottom of your desk right before you got caught with possession; back about the time I began to sense that there was a conspiracy surrounding me to teach me how to read, our town actually had its very own newspaper, called *The Brookline News*. Sheets of strong white paper about the size of an outhouse window, held together with two erratic staples in the cramped left margin, it was reported, printed, distributed and continuously invented by Harold Burgess, the publisher.

The purpose of this newspaper was the same as every paper: to explain what the adults were doing while we kids were busy with our childhoods. In our case, fortunately, the adults were not occupied in murdering, molesting and defrauding each other. Typical headlines: GRANGE FAIR BEING PLANNED, DANCING LESSONS SCHEDULE ANNOUNCED, BROOKLINE FOLKS ENJOY CRUISE, BICYCLE REGISTRATION PLATES HAVE ARRIVED. A front page news story would read like this one of February, 1959:

RODNEY WRIGHT CATCHES 7½
POUND 28 INCH LAKE TROUT

Rodney Wright, Larry Corey, Edith Corey and Franklin Marshall, each caught their limit of lake trout while fishing through the ice at Lake

*Winnipesaukee last Tuesday. Eight fish were
caught by the group, the smallest of which was
nineteen inches.*

This is front page news we dream of seeing again some-
day. Two months later, *The Brookline News* carried this article on page five, reported here verbatim:

*We hear that Edna Reed was chased by a
dogrecently while walking one of the streets of
our town. We don't know whos dog nor whether
he caught her but for heavens sake Edna, dont
stop in one place too long.*

This is a news article worth a thousand words, though it
might seem unimportant to some. It is historic, because it
exhibits the first flicker of the dawn of punctuation in *The
Brookline News*. Notice the smart apostrophe in the first
"don't." It also tells you about life in our little town: it was a
town where dogrecentlys roamed free, and a town where
people liked to walk. Edna Reed happened to be our next
door neighbor, but everyone else in town would know exactly who she was and why it was funny that she should be
chased by a dogrecently.

It was some years off before that most serious of political
debates that comes at last to every knot of human beings
would come to Brookline: the debate over dogs and
leashes, those coequal threats to a happy community. We
were still in our golden age. And we still had a sense of humor.

Of course, there were some hard news items as well,
such as how much money was made by the church fair,
who was running for governor, an occasional car accident
or natural disaster, the ball field getting cut up by horses,
and so on. Letters to the editor usually explained the evils
of communism to the still uninformed, and a column called
"The Chatterbox" was written by A. Nonymous, and held

the latest gossip about teenagers, using initials to disguise their names:

> *Hey, A.W. that was a pretty good way of getting out of school!!!! That was good spaghetti Saturday night, too bad certain boys weren't their to enjoy the party!!! H.B. is still making daily trips to Hollis. Anyone want a ride???? C.S. must be the outdoor type!!!!!!!*

What did it matter if we mixed up "their" and "there"? It was all ours. Harold Burgess may not have subscribed to the theory that "no news is good news." The rest of us not only subscribed to it, but had an even better theory: very *small* news is good news, and the tiniest news is the best news. Our news was monumentally small, extraordinary in how ordinary it was. If you didn't know how to read yet, you didn't miss a thing.

Cigarettes and Boiled Potatoes

Not long after the end of World War II, my father gave up smoking and took up starting a family. Right after he polished off his final cigarette, he put the remains of the pack in a bureau drawer where he kept it for fifteen years, waiting for a certain moment.

During the war he had been a pilot, flying gigantic bombers on test missions. When he wasn't flying, he was courting my mother by airmail and ground mail. Here is a sample of one of the many letters he wrote to her:

> *There we were, traveling through the sky at 200 miles per hour – twenty-two people and myself. The hostess had just served the noon meal and all was quiet and peaceful. Then it happened!*
>
> *Mr. A's fork slipped slightly and a boiled potato shot through the air, striking Mr. B directly between the eyes. Mr. B immediately made the statement that although he was fond of boiled potato, he didn't like it served up in that manner, and who the hell did Mr. A think he was throwing his food around like that at the other passengers. Mr. A then said he was sorry, but come to think of it, if the potato was going to hit anyone between the eyes, he was glad it turned out to be Mr. B; and would Mr. B please return his potato. This, Mr. B gladly did.*
>
> *As soon as Mr. A had wiped enough of the potato out of his eyes to see red again, he jumped to his feet, rolled up his sleeves and asked Mr. B if he would care to step outside for a minute and settle the argu-*

ment; whereupon Mr. B said he would be delighted.
The two of them stepped out, arguing violently, and
immediately all was quiet and peaceful again.

We do not know which gentleman was the victor, but
we are satisfied that they had ample opportunity to air
their feelings towards each other.

Sometime during this courtship, my mother was riding to the movies in a Ford my father was driving along Main Street in Concord, New Hampshire on an icy winter evening. The road was slick. My father saw a parking space on the other side of the street. He stepped on the gas, put the car into a skid, slid around facing in the opposite direction and skated sideways into the space, stopping neatly between two parked cars. My mother decided on the spot that she had to marry this guy.

So that's how we came to be, and fifteen years after my father smoked his last pack of cigarettes we were lying on the big double bed in my parents' bedroom, where we used to sprawl out to watch westerns on the black and white TV set. It was a Saturday morning and my father must have been tracking some strange rumblings and rumors about my older brother Ted. I expressed some curiosity too, and so my father decided the certain moment had come at last.

"You've tried a cigarette, Ted? But did you do it right? And *you* want to know what they taste like too?" I must have been about twelve and Ted was two years older than me. "I think I might have a pack around here somewhere," he said, as he opened his bureau drawer and pulled out a package of cigarettes with a label from another era.

He lit one up for each of us. Ted took a drag and my father pointed out that he hadn't inhaled it and explained the method. Ted inhaled, and quickly left the room, spluttering and coughing. Then after another long lecture to me about how you had to get the smoke down into your lungs to enjoy it, I practically sucked the ancient tobacco right out of it and all the way down into my skinny puerile lungs.

I ran to the bathroom and exhaled a very thick cloud of smoke into the septic tank behind our house. I looked in the mirror and saw that I was a deep shade of blue. I gagged and burned and choked and wheezed and coughed for a good long time that morning.

I don't know what my father did after that with the pack of cigarettes, but I never asked for them again, and neither did Ted, and we never asked anyone else again for a cigarette either, to this day. We both have healthy lungs and we don't even care.

Bill Dulac's Tree House

I WAS ABOUT TWO YEARS into my eight best tree-climbing years, but I'd never seen anything like Bill Dulac's tree house. Bill lived a few black-shuttered, white farmhouses below my house on Old Milford Road. My friend Peter Crowell lived further up the road.

Peter and I and David Shedd (whose house was around the corner) knew every clod of territory both on and off that road from Peter's house down to Bill's house. The pine saplings on the wood paths didn't dare poke out their heads because our flying feet passed over so often. The milkweed pods grew up with an overwhelming sense of doom, destined to be squashed by tires on Old Milford Road while six omnipotent eyes and ears watched and listened. The rainwater running down the ditches slowed down of its own volition, knowing it was no match for the junior corps of engineers that had its headquarters there.

So it was a little surprising that I knew nothing about the tree house. One summer afternoon Peter and David and I ambled down the road toward Bill's, breaking ranks only once for a passing two-tone Chevy, and making only one stop, to see how the rhubarb was coming along at Arthur Cook's.

Bill came out and we went behind his house to the tree house. There stood a towering white pine, that looked like it had grown to its immense size with a will to embrace the whole world and all of childhood too. Its arms were many and strong and supple. It was a tree that wanted to give itself, that welcomed the busy race of boys, along with the birds and raccoons and squirrels. I looked up along a thick knotted rope and saw the bottom of a multi-storied tree house, whose top was hidden in the green boughs at a dizzying height. We climbed up a ladder and entered the lowest story.

Four of us sat comfortably on the gray wooden floor, amid a variety of nailheads emerging like mushrooms. We talked and we told stories. Peter sang us his favorite song: *Dirty L'il, dirty L'il, Lives on top of garbage hill, Never washes, never will, KWICK POO, Dirty Li'l.*

We all tried it, with our individual expectoration simulations, some more real than others. I kept looking at the door in the ceiling. When I got too curious the others seemed to try to discourage me. But after a while they let me climb through with them into a second floor almost as roomy and comfortable as the first. It was a long time before they took me through the trap door in *that* ceiling, and then there were several weeks of initiation, mostly jumping out of the tree hanging onto the knotted rope, before they took me up through the door into the fourth story, where I looked longingly toward yet another door above me.

Is this memory real? Perhaps it is only a memory of one of those multiple-room dreams that haunt us all our lives. But I seem to remember a tree house of at least five stories, made of every shape and size of wood and other material that served the purpose. Some of it was painted, some not. It looked like it had taken many years of inspiration and accretion to build. It was a ramshackle monument, a lot like civilization.

When the day came at last that I was permitted to enter the penthouse, I had a sense of exhilaration and triumph, but it lasted only a moment. This last room was too small and too far from where things happened. No one sat there and sang *Dirty L'il* or told stories. It was too ethereal for that, too heady. So I spent the rest of my days in the bottom floor with my friends. Here we were close to the earth. We picked at our dirty fingernails while we displayed the meager contents of our brains amid the mushrooming nails.

That enormous pine tree is still there by the Dulac's house, although it has long since spilled the boards and memories back into the earth, along with many of the branches that once held us up. I see the tree as I drive by on Old Milford Road. I note that it is old and tired now, not so sure if it should have given so much; not so confident of what boys might do, but ready, I think, to do it all over again if it had to.

Uncle Elwood

Whichever Uncle Elwood drove up in his long station wagon with wood-panelled sides, we were waiting anxiously in the gravel driveway. It was a beautifully clear Saturday in autumn. My three older brothers and my younger sister stood enjoying the morning sunshine on their faces, while I hung close beside my father, my head only a little higher than his waist.

"I've been wanting to do this for years," said my father, as much to himself as to the rest of us. When Uncle Elwood climbed from his car, his legs were so long that his belt buckle seemed nearly as high as the roof of the car. He stood up as straight as he could, and a tiny breeze raised a feather of white hair on his head. He was wearing a white short-sleeved summer shirt that had the same texture as one of my grandfather's shirts. Uncle Elwood was a water-magician.

My father, who was an engineer by training, knew how almost everything worked. (It was maddening how he always one-upped you when you were trying to fix something.) It was only natural that he would take a very skeptical view of the occult science of dowsing. But in my father's teeming brain, curiosity battled it out relentlessly with common sense. Curiosity almost always won the day. We knew it was only a matter of time before he would put Uncle Elwood to the test.

A week earlier, Uncle Elwood had divined a site for the well that would supply water to the new school. While school board members and townfolk looked on, he paced the ground with a forked hazel twig in his upturned palms. When the stick veered and pointed sternly into the earth, he made his prediction: a vein of water would be found at 115 feet, that would flow at a rate of 15 gallons per minute. They took extra care to level the drilling rig. They hit water at exactly 115 feet and got a flow of 14 gallons per minute. This conquest became a front page article in the town's newspaper, with a photograph of Uncle Elwood drinking water from a garden hose connected to the new well. The caption read MMMM Good. I think it was this news story that led to my father's invitation.

Uncle Elwood showed us several of his weird Y-shaped divining sticks. He took one made of willow and walked around our yard. He explained that he wasn't sure if it turned by itself or if he turned it involuntarily with muscle spasms when he received an unconscious message from a subterraneous source.

Then my father stationed us, one just outside the cellar door behind the house, one in earshot of the first, two more across the side and front of the house and one in the middle of the road that passed in front of our house, where Uncle Elwood stood waiting with his willow stick. There was a pipe that passed under the road to supply our house with water and my father could turn the flow of water on or off down in our cellar. Uncle Elwood was to tell us when it was on and when it was off.

"On—off—off—off—on—off, he augured, as word got passed down the line to the cellar, where the hair on the back of my father's neck was beginning to rise. This went on for quite some time and Uncle Elwood didn't bungle once. To us, this was science at its best.

A little panicked, but well satisfied too, we all took turns holding the twig and trying to dowse, while Uncle Elwood stooped low to show us how to do it. It didn't work for any of us except my older brother Tom, who was amazed that the stick turned down for him over the same veins that Uncle Elwood found.

Years later, as I sat in a college classroom thousands of miles from home, I read Hamlet's famous words, speaking to his friend while the ghost of his father lurked offstage: *There are more things in heaven and earth, Horatio, than are dreamt of in our philosophy.* Suddenly, I saw the white clapboard New England house where I grew up. Then I thought of woods and of wood itself, and of willow trees. In my imagination, I sipped the best well water in the world, and I saw clearly, with the eyes that can't be seen, Uncle Elwood.

Home for Good

WE COULD HAVE LEFT HER in the rest home. Everyone was selling the concept: doctors, nurses, relatives, magazines. But something told my mother not to listen. Even as my grandmother sat visiting at our table, and we could all see that she was what we call a "vegetable," my mother announced firmly that we were bringing her home to live out her old age with us.

The reason was simple: as my father's mother, she was responsible for my father's sense of humor. When she laughed, her face got so contorted and pulled in so many directions at once that it looked like it was going to disintegrate. Her facial muscles could never keep a good joke in its place. Once, when my father was a boy, she told him he had to have everything in his room hung up by the time she came home from a shopping trip. He pounded nails into the ceiling and hung up every table and chair, even the bed. She started to be angry with him. Then her face got the better of her.

Another time she told him there wasn't a box of chocolates hidden in her bureau drawer, though he had just seen it. He ate all the chocolates. When she found the empty box, he said, "You were right; there isn't a box of chocolates in your drawer." Her face lost again. A good joke was closely allied with her sense of justice.

My mother's other reason for bringing "Grammy" home was that she had once made the most famous doughnuts at Merrymount, our place on Lake Winnipesaukee. When word went out, dozens of children and adults from around the shoreline showed up in Grammy's kitchen and pilfered the doughnuts off the brown paper bag before they were really cool enough to grab. We walked out tossing them in the air and blowing on them. When my mother married my father and he asked her to replicate his mother's doughnuts, she made some that were so substantial he took them out and used them for target practice. They shattered into a thousand pieces when he hit one mid-air, and she never made doughnuts again.

So Grammy sat there at the table, drugged and unable to move, talk or feed herself, and my mother insisted that she was going to bring her home for good. She did. She replaced the drugs with attention, and Grammy came back to life and filled many years of our childhood with the overbrimming wine of old age. It's hard to say who gained the most from those years.

Once, as Grammy backed up slowly to get into her rocking chair, she underestimated the distance and sat down on the floor with a thud. She looked up at us, then lifted her arm and snapped her fingers, as if to say, "Darn, missed!" And then her face lost all control again.

Like my own childhood, her old age couldn't say everything it knew. Halfway as I am through my own journey, I remember another episode from those years:

Good

She liked her tea-party when she was old,
Old and full of a universe of thought
Our ears and eyes were too weak to reach.
Or else her words hung on their gray branch
Long after the others had died and dropped,
Persistent oak leaves, or stubborn as beech.
It wasn't either late, or long from lunch

When she and mother and sister and I stopped
Whatever we did, and sat around the table.
Our clear well-water weathered cold to hot
While mother showed her the Constant Comment label.
That was all she wanted to be told.

Once, on a barren winter afternoon,
Cozy, as we settled around the pot,
Sister effused, "This tea is awful good."
Followed by my mother, "Yes, this tea
Is awful good." There the comment stood
A long while, before it came to me,
And I saw it waiting, and I said, "Yes,
This tea is awful good." And we thought
We'd reached the end, when suddenly she
Shook her thin lips and said, "Yes, this tea
Is awful…" and in her eyes soon
Came the light that should have been the word
That stayed, the word impossible to miss
That she was still afraid we hadn't heard.

Crime and the Chicken House

"**I**'M NOT GOING TO wear them!"

"Oh yes you are!"

"I'm not going to school if you make me wear them!"

"Oh yes you are!"

"They're the ugliest things I've ever seen. *Nobody* wears those any more!"

"Yes they do. *We* do!"

"I *hate* those rubbers. I'm not wearing them and I mean it. I really *mean* it."

And with that I seized the thick brown molded rubbers my mother was holding out and pulled them with trembling fingers and shaking hands over my brown lace shoes, storming out our barn door and down the gravel driveway to begin a half-mile walk to school on a misty New England morning.

I tramped through barely perceptible puddles along the edge of the road and turned the corner by the Reed's house, the big house that was next door to ours. I kept muttering to myself: "Evidently she doesn't know I'm a sixth-grader yet, or else that just doesn't make any difference to her." Suddenly a strange and mutinous idea broke into my head like an enemy soldier bursting into a house.

I looked carefully to see if Mrs. Reed was watching out her window. When I didn't see her, I took the rubbers off swiftly, ran up to a large bush that crowded against the white clapboards on the side of her house, slipped the rubbers deftly underneath it and kept on walking, as though I had only stopped to look at a caterpillar.

In a town that can still measure its population with three digits, you have to be careful of every little thing you do. Insurrectionists find it's hardly worth the bother, not because of any moral inhibition, but just because every crime is discovered practically the moment it happens and reported to the home authorities, i.e. parents, almost before the criminal can get home himself. I had seen many examples of this in my town.

One time my older brother Ted was wandering through the center of town with a couple of his alleged friends. They stopped behind someone's house to study the architecture of an abandoned chicken house. They noticed that many of the small windows were already broken, but that there were still a fair number of unbroken windows. The shed had not been occupied for years, so they didn't see any real need for those unbroken windows, and they subdued them quickly with stones.

My brother Ted could run fast. But not quite as fast as Rumor can make it across a small town. By the time Ted got home, Rumor had already been there, and my mother knew that a very angry chicken-house owner was on his way to talk to her. What was amazing about all this was not the severity of the crime or the punishment (hard labor for Ted and his friends for three afternoons), but the swiftness with which the crime was reported and tried and a sentence handed down. Justice was done almost before the stones began their downward slide into the panes of glass.

It's hard to understand what made me think I could turn to a life of crime under these circumstances. I was edgy all the way to school. I had never managed to keep my feet so dry as I did that morning. I was fidgety behind my desk all day. My penmanship lesson went terribly. After school, I practically ran home. When I got to the Reed's house, I searched again for witnesses. I didn't see any. I rushed up to the bush.

My close-cropped hair stood almost on end when I looked and couldn't find the brown rubbers anywhere. After casually leaning round and examining every bush for strange creatures of any sort, I finally gave up and dragged myself defeated home. As I entered through the barn and into the mud room I saw the brown rubbers neatly lined up in their usual place. I went inside and found my mother having tea with a visitor I'd seen many times, whose name started with a big R. By the time my mother had said hello and politely asked me about my day at school, I had already reevaluated my future.

My Father's Business Trips

ONE CRISP SEPTEMBER afternoon I sailed my bike down Old Milford Road, jibed dangerously into our driveway, and hove into our barn where I made my bike fast against the floor. I ducked past our green and white Chevy with the "I Like Ike" sticker on the back window and ran into the house. My father had just returned from a three-day business trip. There were four small boxes lined up on the dining room table.

I think my father's undercover rationale for his business trips was to gather new toys which he pretended to give to us when he got back: skateboards, pogo sticks, musical instruments, games, mazes and gadgets of every kind. They all had a couple of things in common; they were so well made that they lived in our barn for many years, and they were original.

It was Friday. Two days of being cast peacefully adrift from the shores of good hygiene and mental application loomed large ahead of us. We were naturally anxious to rip open the boxes. We threw them on the floor as we hauled out our treasures. We all had the same thing. I studied mine and was puzzled. It was a bright silver cylinder, like a little jet engine, about four inches in diameter with blades inside that were connected to a shaft that stuck out from the smaller end. It had a silver chain attached to a black ring that circled it.

My father's explanation thrilled me. You attached it to the front wheel-fork of your bike with the chain stretched up to the handlebars. The shaft rubbed against the tire when you pulled on the chain. They were *sirens*. They were built for volume and they should have been illegal. No more lowly cardboard-in-the-spokes for us. These were as close to real sirens as you would ever get without growing up to be a policeman.

It was a big year for sirens and alarms. Every few weeks, it seemed to me, we stopped what we were doing to listen to the air raid siren, an eerie sound to be born in the middle of the day in a small New England town. We paused to think about our bomb shelters, whether they were well-stocked with enough Campbell's soup and enough aspirin to cure the severe headaches caused by nuclear bombs. Then we went back to playing and working.

We payed close attention to sirens in those days. There were many nights when I pelted into my parents' big double bed and listened through the dark windows to the sirens whooping through the town, guessing at their distance and direction and waiting for the results of my father's calls to various friends. There was no such thing as turning a deaf ear to a siren, the way I almost managed to do when I grew older and lived in a city. On a cold New England night, sirens sent shivers of apprehension and gratitude up and down your spine.

So it was no surprise that bolting these babies onto the fronts of our bikes would bring us a kind of pleasure unlike any other. Even better, since we lived on Old Milford Road, we could huff and puff all the way up to Sonny Farwell's house, which was a few miles, and then come screeching down, pulling the chain all the way, flying dangerously over the heaved-up road with only one hand on the handlebars.

We got our sirens shrieking so loud and so high for so many accumulated miles that half the town of Brookline was probably filled with anxiety, while only a lucky few of our immediate neighbors were merely annoyed. I can still feel the wind racing past my ringing ears, and I can still feel my chest rising with self-importance. I couldn't wish my friends or rivals to be any more impressed than they must have been.

Unfortunately, after almost a year of this, the fine people at our end of town stopped being impressed. My parents got tired of fielding calls from folks who wanted to know whether someone's house had burned down or the Hall boys were just out riding their bikes again. The police began to get harassing calls from confused citizens.

One day Alvin Taylor, the chief-of-police, knocked on our front door and spoke softly to my father. It was too confusing, he informed him, to have so many ersatz emergencies happening, and would we please stop using those sirens. My father agreed and we ceased from that day, but we kept them on our bikes for looks, and pulled the chains when we were only going fast enough for a purr.

A Four Leaf Clover

I SAT; I PUT HANDS TO KEYS, and I magicked the room. The yellow and white wallpaper uncurled new ears along the seams. My older brother Ted passed through like a specter, floating from one heavy, white, four-paneled, dog-scratched-at-the-bottom door to another one freshly painted but for a holiday in the lower left panel.

My music was astonishing, most of all to me. It felt like I had four, even six hands, each one free as a bird weaving in and out of the flock, one of them out front of the rest twilling and twittering tirelessly. On his passage through the room Ted was magicked without even meaning to be, and far off in the kitchen my mother had a smile on her face and hummed along nearly on key.

It wasn't just my hands. My whole being was deeply involved in this performance of my life. Especially my feet, which were pumping away at the pedals with the energy and velocity of a Horowitz. With those feet, with my magic floating hands, and with my heart swelling and beating like a marathon runner's, I blew the cold New Hampshire air in the little living room right out through the closed windows, and filled the room with warm Mississippi moonlight.

I threw a lever with my left hand and rewound the moonlight until it vanished with a clack, clack, clack, clack, clack. Then I picked up a box that said Q•R•S #8345 and *I'm Looking Over a Four Leaf Clover* on one end. I loaded the roll into the dark hollow on the front of the piano, got it pumping along the tracks, and read the words tumbling in blue syllables down the right hand edge of the paper gliding in front of me: *I'm look-ing o-ver a four leaf clo-ver, that I o-ver looked be-fore. One leaf is sun-shine, the sec-ond is ...* Just then my father came in, peered over my shoulder and started singing along.

If you know anything about my family by now, you know who fetched this player piano home. The man who was forever responsible for us being born, but never responsible for us being bored. He bought it from the Grange, for five dollars, because it didn't work, along with a hundred piano rolls for a hundred dollars. He found eight healthy neighbors under eighteen who had biceps and rolled-up shirt-sleeves and moved the mammoth black piano from the town hall into a pick-up truck and from there into our living room with the yellow and white wallpaper.

Slowly it expanded into the whole room. After a few months, when it was finally a piano again, most of it worked, but the pedals were much too hard to pump. So my father disconnected the bellows and hooked up the blower end of an old vacuum cleaner in their place. The noise of the vacuum mixing with the Mississippi moonlight got to be annoying, so we moved the piano to the front hall, where my father put a hole through the floor, stuck a long hose through and put the vacuum cleaner down there in the cellar, with a wire running back up to a switch mounted on the front of the piano. The vacuum roared in the bowels of our house while we danced and sang to *The Battle of New Orleans* and our front hall drove on relentlessly *from the mighty Mississippi to the Gulf of Mexico.*

But we always longed to use those pedals. It seemed just too easy. Art without sweat. Eventually we disconnected the vacuum cleaner, and moved the piano back into the living room. My father got the pedals working like a quadriceps training machine set to simulate Heartbreak Hill. We couldn't grip the front edge of the piano tightly enough to get any leverage on our legs or to keep from tipping over backwards on the piano bench. So my father attached a heavy seat belt to the front of the piano. With the seat belt cinched up snug behind our backs, we finally got down to the business of making memories. We had many years of use out of the piano and learned hundreds of her rolls by heart.

So what if the words were more from my father's generation than my own. The corniest words are still lodged in my memory like they were my own children: *One leaf is sunshine, the second is rain; third is the roses that grow in the lane. No use explaining, the one remaining is somebody I adore. I'm looking over a four leaf clover, that I overlooked before.*

The Morning After

IT WAS OCTOBER. OUR country was shivering awake from a nightmare. Khrushchev had announced after a very tense week that the missiles would be withdrawn from Cuba. Kennedy's naval quarantine had been successful. The country shook her towering head in disbelief and gratitude that she had stepped so close to the nuclear monster without rousing him up. Of course, we kids didn't know what all the fuss was about, and our parents clinging to the black and white TV forgot that in a few days they would be faced by an even worse nightmare, one far more tangible to them: Halloween was about to hit town.

There was a certain youthful, orgiastic attitude toward Halloween in those days, and a widespread and severely misplaced trust in kids on the part of grown-ups. Parents were not expected to cruise around in vans delivering their children to doorstoops and eavesdropping on what went into their bags. Their job was to stay home dispensing caramel popcorn balls while all hell broke loose in town. They were expected to accept this role humbly, and hope their children survived.

Our Chief of Police, Alvin Taylor, had declared that Halloween would be celebrated on Wednesday night only, and that no vandalism would be tolerated. That meant that my best friend David Shedd and I had to develop our plan the weekend before.

One of the two haunted houses in town was on a hill rising abruptly behind the church steeple, overlooking the main street of town. That Saturday, David and I were creeping around the hilltop as close to the house as we dared to go, when we discovered a tree with an enormous cavity in it, overhanging the edge of the steep bank. That was it. We had our plan. We went back to his house and got two big burlap bags.

We filled the bags with rotten apples from the two lone apple trees that stood dying in the middle of the Shedd's field. We hauled the heavy bags through the woods to the hollow tree and carefully stocked in the apples, our ammunition for Halloween. We did the same thing again on Sunday. The church and the tiny fire station stood next to each other on Main Street, and there was a clear line of sight between them as we looked over the steep bank down to the street and the sidewalk far below. Our plan was to chuck apples down all night on the people and the cars passing by.

The next two days at my house, my brothers and I checked the dried pea supply in our cabinets, while the five kids in the Shedd family dug out their two oversize suitcases to have ready for candy storage. They were serious candy collectors. Traditionally, they blitzed the town, pooled it all, filled the two huge suitcases to their brims and kept them under a bed, from where they dispensed candy to themselves and their friends for months afterward.

Halloween night came. The church bells in both churches rang out, little breaking-and-entering devils swinging from the ropes. Bands of vulgar apparitions in dungarees and beat-up shoes roamed the dark streets with pea shooters and bags full of peas, waiting to get into a war with other bands. Rolls of toilet paper flew like despondent ghosts over telephone wires. The town's inventory of bathroom supplies, like soap and shaving cream, was severely depleted in a few hours. Weird, Armageddon shapes appeared on the surfaces of windowpanes all over town.

David and I sat in the dark in our eagle's nest, hurling our apples down.

A twinge of conscience made us decide to forego the cars and concentrate on the sidewalk instead. Another twinge made us begin to intentionally aim at the gaps between people instead of at their heads. But that didn't diminish the fun any. We kept up an almost steady hail of apples for two hours.

In the quarantine of morning I walked to school through the war-torn town, and saw the carnage everywhere, including the gruesome white pulp and red skin on the sidewalk between the firehouse and the church. I was impressed and embarrassed. I walked straight through it without looking down, and I never looked back.

Good Heavens, Mrs. Hall

THERE WERE SEVEN OF US against the chill November. We sat around the voluminous dining room table, a red cloth covering the dark wood that bore the scratches and lines and circles of many years of homework pressed unmindfully into its surface. My father forked slabs of corned beef onto plates for three older brothers, a younger sister, finally me, and then my mother and himself. My mother filled unbreakable dark green bowls with enormous wedges of cabbage and passed them around the table. Outside, the wind flung handfuls of leaves against the screen door separated from our dining room only by a cold front porch.

Our house was minimally heated by oil, but it was brought up to comfort by the abundance of food, the confusion of conversation, and my father's sense of humor. My father grabbed the butter, the vinegar and the salt and pepper and put them affectionately onto his cabbage. "Ooh baby," he said, "my favorite." We all copied him and then began to eat. My father took his first bite. "Ooh baby. It's got that *Je ne sais quoi*," he said, smacking his lips, "but I don't know what it is." One older brother laughed.

We were still eating when a knock came on the door. I ran to open it, and there on the front porch stood a rather small older man with an oversize briefcase in one hand. He swept a thin tuft of hair up over his forehead and said, "Good evening, is this the Hall household? I'm from the encyclopedia."

There was a reason for this. My mother had received a present from her father of $200, an enormous sum in 1961. One day she was trying to decide how to spend it while she sat leafing through a magazine. She came across an ad for the Encyclopedia Britannica and she sent in a coupon for more information. A week later this man showed up at our door at dinner time. "Good *heavens!*" he said, "You're still eating."

My mother really *was* anxious to have a dependable source of knowledge located somewhere within the boundaries of our town, and so she invited the man in, even though she was quite embarrassed about being in her bathrobe and nightie. He was an unlikely Willy Loman. Not only did he lack the slick energy of your better salesmen, but he was actually a gentleman, and genuinely seemed to care more about getting to know us than he did about selling us an encyclopedia.

We finished up eating, cleared the table, pulled the tablecloth off and all eight of us sat examining glossy brochures and the beautifully bound samples of the encyclopedia, dark maroon with black cobwebs pressed in, and gold stamping. When they came round to me, I was almost overwhelmed by the smell of the binding glue and fresh covers. Unfortunately, something about the whole scene put my father into very rare form, and it was hard to get him serious about anything. "Good *heavens,*" the salesman exclaimed, "what a family!"

"It takes a living heap, to make a house a home," said my father.

"Good *heavens,*" said the salesman.

The conversation went round and round our personal lives, and occasionally it touched on encyclopedias. It got incessantly knocked off its compass by my father's jokes.

He was like a cat playing with the needle arm on a record player, who won't scare down when you yell at him. It was a very scratched conversation. The salesman exclaimed "Good heavens!" more and more frequently and that made my father even more flighty. We hadn't had so much fun in a long time, including the salesman, who seemed to keep forgetting why he was there. The dark table almost levitated with our laughter. My mother was leaning back in her chair too much, and we all kept reminding her not to do that.

Finally, after one of my father's remarks, she leaned back so far, she went over backwards. Her legs flew straight up toward the ceiling out of her bathrobe and nightie. "Good *heavens*, Mrs. Hall," the salesman shouted as he jumped to his feet at the other end of the table. This was the *coup de grâce* that finally convulsed us all, and it took us a while to run to my mother and lift her and the chair up off the floor. She came out of it unblemished.

Of course, we bought the encyclopedia and it served us well for years of homework and settling disputes, like was Tutankhamen married, and cases like that. There was no one in our family who could take a volume down from the shelf without shouting "Good *heavens*, Mrs. Hall!" This went on for many years. Those "good heavens" are where my father is now, with the salesman, but the maroon encyclopedias are still around, stacked on their sides in the back of the barn, waiting for another taker.

"*Then another strip of blue tape and below that: LEIGH, TOM, TED, SID. Years later MARY was added, in a different typeface.*"

PEGBOARDS AND CHECKBOOKS

"*Our bright white farmhouse with glossy black shutters stood in the sunshine at the bottom of a gently rising road.*"

SCOOTERS AND SKATEBOARDS

"My mother decided on the spot that she had to marry this guy."

Cigarettes and Boiled Potatoes

"Slowly it expanded into the whole room."
A Four Leaf Clover

"His character was very well developed, with the help of two grapefruit…"
Barnacle Bill the Sailor

"Immediately we engaged in a reevaluation of our high spirits."
THE BIG BALONEY

"My father wasn't home for dinner, and everyone but Ted and I had managed to get through the liver quagmire and move on."
FINISHING THE DICTAPHONE

"There had been some confusion in my mind…whether she was perhaps Mother Goose herself."

PULL CANDY

"A frail figure in a thin brown coat turned the corner at the store behind me."

CHARLOTTE

The little blue kite that has been seen floating high in the sky over Brookline recently becomes a rather large kite when it is on the ground as shown in the picture above.

Measuring about 10 feet from top to bottom, the kite was built by Sid Hall and his boys with blue nylon cloth being used instead of the conventional paper. Regular string would not stand the tremendous pull when the kite was in the air so a nylon cord was substituted. Approximately 3000 feet of the cord is wound on a wooden reel which is attached to a pipe driven in the ground.

Dancing, was climaxed with a dancing party held on Wednesday, April 18 at the Youth Center.

Mrs. Philip Shattuck, Mrs Alan Haight and Mrs. Frederick Jepson were hostesses for the afternoon intermediate party, and Mrs. Bruce Jones and Mrs. Robert Wright for the evening Junior High Group. Mrs. Alpha Hall and Mrs. Charles Rut-

FIRE EXTINGUISHER
SERVICING
Refilling rates for
CO 2 Extinguishers
20 Ounce....$1.50

"We soon realized that nothing named 'string' would keep this kite tethered to the planet."

THE KITE

"'Your brother Ted and Bruce Jones and them – all smoke ciggies up in the pine grove, you know,' Peter pronounced as we pedaled our fat bikes…"

FIRE IN THE PINE GROVE

"*There is nothing to do here but what the body wants, and so there is plenty. Generations come and go.*"

NEW HAMPSHIRE

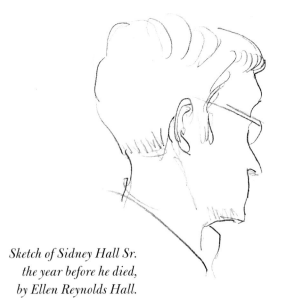

*Sketch of Sidney Hall Sr.
the year before he died,
by Ellen Reynolds Hall.*

The Wind on the Other Side

IT WAS HARD TO FATHOM why we should give thanks. Only a week earlier my father was putting the finishing touches on some upstairs rooms before the whole family came home for Thanksgiving. He had a sudden heart attack, and after a few tense hours of trying not to believe the unbelievable, we finally had to. It was as if gravity ceased to work. The center of our lives suddenly disappeared.

We passed the white sweet potatoes around and talked of my father. We tried to keep bright for our children, but they did more to keep us bright. After the dishes were cleared and washed, we sat around listening to some recordings my father had made years earlier on a Sony reel-to-reel tape recorder. He had managed to use the multiple track feature in a singular way.

We listened to a sweet tenor voice speaking, along with a stride bass on the piano: *Now, I got a gal by the name of Sue...* It kept going as the song began, in perfect three-part harmony: *I got a gal named Sue, and she is a working girl too. She's the chief engineer in the nightshirt factory. There's nothing that she can't do. Her phone is all she had. She got a face like a soft-shell crab. And every night she used to tussle with the button on her bustle. Oh my Susie was bad.*

"The Dummy Line," "Minnie the Mermaid." His infectious, impeccable singing and whistling and harmonizing. Then a trip through the jungle with birds and beasts. A blood-curdling version of "The Congo," with me beating on a drum. Finally a recitation of "The Highwayman," with me doing sound effects and both of us trying not to laugh. *Her musket shattered the moonlight.* "Pop," goes my father, with his finger in his mouth when I fail to supply the effect.

I'm standing beside my grandparents' dining room table near the big sliding wooden doors that go into the living room, in their enormous house in Concord, New Hampshire. I'm wearing my best shirt, and reciting every verse of *Over the river and through the wood, to grandmother's house we go.* When I'm done, everyone applauds. I sit and we begin to eat. Someone passes me the white sweet potatoes. I ask for the gravy.

I'm in Norwich, Vermont at my aunt and uncle's house, our second childhood home. Uncle John is carving the turkey. The conversation soon turns to politics and the Vietnam War. My family is liberal on most every issue. My uncle is very conservative, and when he's not conservative enough he takes the other side anyway, just for the pleasure of it. We're never sure exactly what he believes. Some of us relish the political debate; some keep trying to get beyond it, or ahead of it again. I pass my potato skins to Uncle John, just before he says, "The skins are my favorite part. Of course, you know that already."

We decide to go outside afterwards for a game of football, even though the back yard has just had a dusting of the year's first snow. "Tatch or Tuckle?" my father asks, a phrase that gets repeated for years to come, although he claims he really *did* mean to say, "Touch or tackle?" In the middle of the game, my father invents a new play. My older brother Ted was well known for his ability to pump up his stomach until he looked nine months pregnant. He once got kicked out of Latin class for blowing it up with an imaginary squeeze bulb and lifting it onto his desk in the middle of a lesson. After our huddle, we fake a pass to Ted who expands his stomach and pretends to be hiding the ball under his shirt. While he gets pummeled by the other team, my father scores a touchdown carrying the ball nonchalantly nestled against his red plaid shirt.

We are home again in Brookline. There are about fifteen of us. An enormous turkey sits before my father. On the table are bowls of stuffing, and white sweet potatoes, and baby onions in cream sauce, and pitchers of gravy, and celery sticks stuffed with blue cheese, and dishes of bright red cranberry sauce, and apple cider, and, waiting in the kitchen, pumpkin and apple pies. The heavy door between the dining room and the windy front porch is closed, a cluster of Indian corn hanging on a nail on the other side of it. It has been there for many years.

My mother brings in the good china plates. They haven't had time to warm up from the cold barn room where they were stored. My father carefully heats each one with an old hair dryer before he puts the slabs of turkey on. We're laughing and we forget to say grace. We forget to say what we are thankful for. I ask for the white sweet potatoes and someone holds them out to me. I say thank-you, and then I ask for the gravy.

Black Box

EVERYTHING WAS WHITE. The snow drove in almost horizontally from the northeast. The white clapboards and black shutters of our house were barely visible. The black screens and the white gingerbread trim of the front porch were spattered with heavy clumps of snow. In the driveway the Chevy truck was almost buried. The robust skeleton of a maple tree and the wires that ran from the street to the house were visible only as ghostly gray lines. The big black barn door was closed tight; the row of small window panes above it looked gray and lost, like the windows of a ship in a storm.

Two of my older brothers and I, wearing ski parkas tied at the throats and hoods pulled over our hats, and ski goggles that covered most of our faces, made our way to the back yard, where we pushed in a line through the snow that was up to my chest and almost to theirs. It was gorgeous, light and fluffy, but soon became heavy enough to stay in place as we dug a whole network of tunnels that connected to one big room in the center of the yard.

The stonewall at the back of our property dropped off abruptly into the neighboring field. My brother Ted and I stood side by side on the buried wall. We lowered our goggles and dove off in tandem. The snow swallowed us. We came up mostly white, and Ted patted me twice on the head.

The "freak snowstorm" of 1960 lived in our memories for many years, not only because it dumped over three feet of snow all at once, but because we had it on film. My father had a square black box of a camera, that somehow managed to take home movies worth seeing. My mother's father had bought the black box in 1929 and given it to my parents when they got married. Thirty years old, it was still taking great pictures. After sixty years, it did just as well, and it would today, if you could afford the 16 millimeter film for it, and if you applied my father's philosophy of picture-taking, which, I think, boiled down to "Never take anything but action shots."

One busy Christmas, he had someone take a picture of him reading a newspaper as he walked through a door next to a dart board on the wall. Then the camera panned to a group of boys throwing darts, then back to him with a suction-cupped dart stuck on his forehead, his tongue hanging out and his eyes rolling. This type of thing went on for years, so, needless to say, all seven of us in my family spent many hours strewn around the living room listening to the clack of the old projector and watching these silent movies on the snowy white pull-up screen.

That's just what we were doing for the hundredth time with the shots of the freak snowstorm. We all wanted to see Ted's famous solo dive again. As we watched the pictures of snow driving in sideways in front of the black shutters, the skeleton of the maple tree and gray wires behind the snow, the kids wading in the back yard, we were a little disappointed at how dark the pictures were. It was unusual for my father to let the deepest dark of the winter get a foothold on the surface of his film. In its retelling on the screen, the storm's black and white is taking on a deeper mystery.

Then suddenly there is light, bright yellowish light on the snow. Ted stands on the stonewall with his back to the impending dive. He puts down his yellow-lensed goggles and swings his arms three times, bending his knees with each swing. He lands on his back in the deep snow and disappears from view. There is a very long pause. Finally half a leg with a black rubber boot on it comes up out of the snow and vanishes again. Then two whole legs shoot straight up, splay out and disappear again. Then legs and arms start flailing and appearing and vanishing in every direction.

At last, a bright red hat, and a head and shoulders appear. Ted struggles to his feet and moves toward the camera, his snow-clad body swaying from side to side, as he lifts his goggles from his rosy red cheeks. When he gets close to the camera, the heart-wrenching expression of the saddest of circus clowns arises from the depths of his being and spreads across his face. He comes all the way in for a close-up.

We roar with laughter as my father rewinds and plays this scene again and again. Inwardly we think, how wonderful that our father is not the kind to stop filming to help his son out of the snow. The film flapping through its long loops on the old projector sounds like a small engine popping. The character on the screen never says a word, but we are happy that he is in color.

It Runs in the Family

THE SUMMER AFTER I fiNISHED high school I took a trip to Nova Scotia in a VW Bus with my three older brothers. As we passed through Maine's and Canada's vast wilderness, I answered the call of nature so often that they finally took a picture of my back in the woods just so that later we could all have the Aristotelian pleasure of recognition. My father used to have the same problem. "Handy little thing to take on a picnic," he'd mumble as he came back from the wayside. It runs in the family, you might say.

I was sitting at the fourth desk back, in the row by the wall in Mrs. Varney's fifth grade classroom. Three rows of sixth graders sat on the other side of the room. Mrs. Varney juggled the two classes skillfully. Unfortunately I had to go to the bathroom again. I had already been twice that morning. Mrs. Varney always treated any request to go to the bathroom with a curious mixture of trust and mistrust. She was a model of stern generosity. I didn't want to take advantage of her. Worse than that, I didn't think she would actually believe I had to go again, even if it was the truth. I didn't want to have to walk home from school carrying my lunch box in both hands in front of me. I had to think fast.

I needed to come up with a brilliant lie. Something told me to think of a thing so preposterous that she would *have* to believe me. To doubt me would be to doubt my very integrity. A few preliminary ideas didn't seem to fit the bill even though they were completely preposterous. Finally it came to me that if I had the right physical injury, I could use it as an excuse over and over for a long time to come. It would have the added advantage of evoking sympathy from Mrs. Varney and from any one else if she should happen to make it public.

My first idea was to have all my fingers on my right hand be broken. I started to think of ways this could have happened to me, then realized my hand would be readily visible when I went up to talk to her. But once I had imagined myself this far, it was only one short step to the solution. My toes were well concealed. She wouldn't ask me to take my shoes and socks off in front of the class for verification.

While she was lecturing the sixth graders about coffee plantations in Brazil, I quietly got up out of my seat and approached her desk. I kept the ragged brown shoe on my right foot flat to the hardwood floor as I walked with a very expressive limp. It took longer than usual to get to her desk. I explained to her that I had had a serious accident which had cut off my third toe on my right foot and that they had just brought me home from the hospital where it had been sewn back on. I thought I should go to the bathroom and check on it.

Mrs. Varney looked down at me with a straight face. "Of course," she said, in a kindly voice, as I thought I caught a reflection of two of myself in her horn-rimmed glasses. I started to leave the room, then came back to her, limping deftly. "The doctor and my parents and I all think this should be kept secret," I whispered up to her. "Of course," she said.

I hastily hobbled to the bathroom, relieved at my success. I thought it best to spend extra time in there. I stood and stared vacuously at the white wall, impressed by its phenomenal blandness and the amazing height of the unpainted plastered ceiling above it. I calculated how long it would take to remove a shoe and a sock and then do something or other and then put the sock back on and then the shoe and then tie up the shoe using the speed method. I wasn't a slacker, after all.

Then I reentered the classroom and moved, like a man well accustomed to limping, back to the fourth desk in the row by the wall. I was delighted at my brilliance. There probably was not a more appropriate scheme on the face of the planet. I had taken in Mrs. Varney flat-out. I was able to use this strategy for weeks to come. With only the slightest tilt of my head as I approached her desk, Mrs. Varney would nod and send me off to the bathroom. But it was a high risk deception and eventually I had to tell her I was all better.

Meanwhile, I walked home afternoons warm and dry in the after-school sunlight. Conscience didn't stand a chance against the comfort of this. It was years before a sudden vision of Mrs. Varney made me think about my sleaziness, and even then, the corners of her stern mouth were still turned up, almost into a smile.

White Belts and Finks

B Y THE TIME I MADE IT to Mrs. Varney's sixth grade class, I had worked my way up through the cluttered ranks to the highest position of responsibility a Brookline boy could hope to capture: I was captain of the School Safety Patrol. Let Kennedy and Khrushchev squabble over Cuba and bring the planet close to the brink of destruction. I had more important troubles. I was answerable for the daily operations of a rag-tag troop of thirteen short unseasoned safety patrollers.

Every morning I considered what clothes would look the most spiffy with my white patrol belt. Usually I picked a light blue sweater that had white and black stripes running up both sides of the front zipper and around the collar. It made me look like a Westpointer, I thought. Then I went to the closet and pulled my safety belt carefully down off its hanger.

A two inch wide white band passed over one shoulder and across the chest and attached to another band that fastened around the waist with a buckle. A large badge was pinned on just above heart level. An exemplary belt had to be bleached unbearably white and pressed into one dimension by your mother at least once a week. It had to be free of jelly stains or any other blemish at all times. Putting it on with a twist was blasphemous and worthy of a demerit.

I breathed on the badge and buffed it with the blue sleeve of my sweater, admiring the red insignia that only the captain's badge had. Then I drew the belt on and fastened it, skillfully feeling along it for a twist. I had my older brother check the back side, and took him at his word when he said, "No twists." I walked to school full of self-confidence, and reported for duty on the streets of Brookline as soon as I got near the town hall. The white belt and badge conferred enormous powers on the wearer. You could lead long columns of kids along sidewalks. You could even stand in the middle of the road and stop cars and wave them cool-headedly on again.

By some semi-nepotic coincidence, my very best friend, David Shedd, was a lieutenant. I always had an uneasy feeling there was something immoral in this arrangement. I felt I needed to be extra careful putting down those little blue marks in the demerit book. But Roberta Quigley was a lieutenant too, and Brenda Shattuck was a sergeant. Certainly no involvement in that triangle. My other close friends, Peter Crowell and Frank Ward were lowly foot patrollers with plain black badges. Strange I should feel so guilty about being the captain, when I was as clean as my own haircut, and as obvious to everyone as my big ears.

After a year of keeping my troops in line following the directives that came down from Mrs. Varney and from Chief-of-Police Alvin Taylor, I was shocked one day to learn that two other Davids on the patrol had been chosen to represent us on a trip to Washington D.C.: David McNabb and David Young. Not only was I let down that I wouldn't be going myself, but these two Davids had always intimidated me. They were handsome and tall and self-possessed, everything I wasn't. And I hadn't received a single demerit the whole year and they had two each.

Worse than that, David McNabb pointed out to me after the Washington announcement that I had given a fellow patroller a demerit when the Davids had decided already to keep that kid's infraction a secret. David called me a "fink." The word hit me like a Random House Dictionary. I was paralyzed. I didn't know what to answer and I walked home from school in agony.

I kept this awful burden in my soul for a week, every day trying to think of something worse than a "fink" to call David McNabb. But I couldn't. I hated school that week. I hated recess and I hated both Davids. I finally decided the best thing to do would be to look up the word "fink" in a dictionary and then throw back the real meaning in David's face, demonstrating how ignorant he was and erasing the stigma from myself.

For some reason I couldn't get up the courage to look it up. Finally, after a whole week of dwelling on it, I did. The definition stunned me: David had used the word in exactly the right way. A fink was an informer, just what I was when I put down that poor kid's demerit in the book. So it turned out David had a genius for language along with everything else.

A defeated captain, I didn't talk to either David for weeks, until political fortunes finally brought them back to me and we became friends. That was long after I had glanced at the glossy photo of them in their bright white belts standing on the steps of the Lincoln Memorial with Alvin Taylor and a siege of safety patrollers from all over America. They were practically sitting on Lincoln's knee, and they had huge smiles on their faces.

Pegboards and Checkbooks

SOME VERY ASTUTE SCHOLARS argue that the classical Greeks at the height of their culture produced such orderly and rational works of art because in their daily lives they were completely disorderly and irrational. They were Greeks. This argument makes sense to me. It also reminds me of a work of art my father created at the height of his own culture, something that became known simply as "The Pegboard."

He cut a plain piece of Masonite pegboard into an eighteen inch by twenty-four inch rectangle, and stiffened the back with five strips of wood. Across the top he pasted down twenty labels that he had carefully typed out in upper case letters: FEED JET, MAKE BED, MAKE BED, MAKE BED, MAKE BED, CLEAN ROOM, CLEAN ROOM, CLEAN ROOM, CLEAN ROOM, DUST, VACUUM LIVING ROOM, VACUUM DINING ROOM, EMPTY WASTE BASKETS, CLEAN BATHROOM SINKS, PUT AWAY GROCERIES, PUT OUT MILK BOTTLES, FILL SUGAR BOWLS, SET DINNER TABLE, CLEAR DINNER TABLE, and RINSE DINNER DISHES.

He left one row of holes exposed below these labels and then put a strip of blue tape across the length of the board. Down the left hand side the labels read: MONDAY, TUESDAY, WEDNESDAY, THURSDAY, FRIDAY, SATURDAY, SUNDAY. Then another strip of blue tape and below that: LEIGH, TOM, TED, SID. Years later MARY was added, in a different typeface.

He mounted this under the clock on the wall beside the kitchen table, which sat over two long benches in a nook behind a counter that jutted out into the middle of the kitchen. The counter had a half-circle end to it with bright red shelves built in, a light blue dowel running through all of them for support. The bottom shelf was near the floor at just the right height for Jet to eat her canned food and lap her milk from a heavy plastic bowl. It was her sacred spot. We weren't allowed even to talk to her there.

It is Saturday morning. We are gathered around the kitchen table in our bathrobes and there is much commotion. The bidding is about to begin.

"Four cents for Jet," my father shouts. "Four cents a day to feed Jet. Who wants to start the bidding at four?"

"I do," I raise my arm and yell. My father keeps calling for lower bids and waiting but luckily no one comes forward. He pulls a red peg from next to my name at the bottom of the board and sticks it in the hole under FEED JET. Then he distributes a peg of each color into the four MAKE BED holes and into the CLEAN ROOM holes.

Bidding begins again with DUST, the smallest word but the most hated job on the whole board. Ted goes for the maximum bid, four cents again, and strangely, no one offers to underbid. So it goes across the board until a colored peg is placed under every job. Only a few of them have been bid down. I've got PUT OUT MILK BOTTLES, EMPTY WASTE BASKETS, and CLEAR DINNER TABLE in addition to FEED JET. We figure what our profits will be when our peg rows have filled out by week's end.

No one speaks of the collusive rumblings that spread through the rooms of our rambling house on Friday night, the winks, the price fixing. We all seem to know in our hearts that my mother hears everything behind our backs, but she doesn't let on. Kids who do nothing but pour highly refined sugar into the sugar bowl every day get only two cents a day for their trouble. Kids who want to rinse the dinner dishes, on the other hand, can get as much as twenty cents a day. My mother doesn't seem to mind the expense or the very wide discrepancies between our earnings.

Perhaps she and my father don't mind the payroll because of the unique banking system they have instituted. Every kid has his own check book, three checks to a page with stubs. Real check books, except there is no bank name or account number printed on them. The bank is Mom and Dad. For years I faithfully entered my deposits, and wrote out checks, "Pay to the order of cash" on the few occasions when I needed real money. I admit I also wrote many checks that said: "Pay to the order of Mom," to pay for necessary things like the wear and tear on slammed doors.

So the pegboard hung there on the kitchen wall all week accumulating colored pegs, hung there on the blue kitchen wall for so many years that the labels faded and some of them peeled off and the penciled-in high-bid amount was erased and raised many times. It mostly kept a disorderly, fun-loving family orderly and having fun year after year. When I picture it now in my mind, I don't see visions of dust and vacuum cleaners and baskets of milk bottles. I see the colored pegs. I'm amazed that they kept their bright colors for so many years.

Mrs. Russell and Aunt Bea

THERE WERE TWO THINGS THAT Mrs. Russell and Aunt Bea had in common: their faces and their candy jars. Their faces were engraved with the lines of shrewdness that children can't help but recognize, and criss-crossed with the lines of indulgent love that make children feel comfortable. In the 1960's they were in their last decade and I was only in my second. But we recognized each other bank to bank over the hastening river.

And they both had white shelves built into the wall at child level, with rows of square glass candy jars full of candy. To me these shelves were not just the storage space for important vessels. They were the bright engines of education and delight.

Mrs. Russell was the piano teacher. Once a week my mother drove me across town in our self-important Chevy, then up to the top of Russell Hill to the Russell farmhouse which sat, white and splendid, on the brow of Big Muscatanipus Hill, overlooking the lake and the town, surrounded by fenced pastures of white sheep who were sometimes attacked by roving dogs.

I sat at the shiny upright piano in the corner of Mrs. Russell's living room and muttered "All Cows Eat Grass" and "Good Boys Do Fine Always" and "F-A-C-E" and "Every Good Boy Deserves Fudge," over and over under my breath as I struggled with the persistent hieroglyphs propped in front of me.

After "Long, Long Ago," I peeked up sideways into Mrs. Russell's face, learning to read encouragement while I was learning to read music. She was not the kind of teacher you would find in a Boston conservatory. She was the kind of teacher you would find in a small New Hampshire town in the early 1960's. She was not on the cutting edge of music. She *was* on the cutting edge of character.

After every lesson she led me over to the candy jars and let me help myself. I filled my hand with bright colors, and then waited for my mother, who had been visiting somewhere, to come back to get me. Sure, this candy contract involved bribery and bad teeth, but it also involved wisdom and training the soul. Maybe sometimes goodies *are* good for you.

All of my brothers embodied different philosophies of practicing at home. My oldest brother Leigh put in the exact time he was told to do, and apparently never cheated. My brother Tom wouldn't stop when he had a right to, and went on to become a musicologist. My next older brother Ted could only practice with the help of an egg timer propped next to the music in front of him. The dial clicked loudly through the red minutes, and when the little bell dinged, Ted's hands came up instantly off the piano, usually in the middle of a measure. I admit I made use of the egg timer myself, but I often went so far as to finish the whole piece, even after the clicking had stopped.

My Aunt Bea's candy jars were located in her warm kitchen in Concord, where we often stopped to visit on our trips up north. All I needed to do was tell her some tidbit about my life or help with some easy chore and then I had access to the candy jars. Actually, we all had access anyway, no matter what we did, but we had to wait politely until just before our exit. Then she would mention the candy jars, very casually. I dreaded every time that she might forget.

Aunt Bea was married to a three-star General who brought her breakfast in bed every morning of their married life that he was home from the front. The breakfast tray always had a fresh-cut flower on it, from his flower garden or wherever he could find one.

The lines of Aunt Bea's face played *their* music into my soul year after year until I was almost an adult, right up until the time I looked back at her down the hallway of a hospital and the lines on her face told me she knew she never was going to see me again. Those are the lines that will stay with me the longest.

After Mrs. Russell retired, we were sent to another piano teacher at a music store in Nashua, the largest nearby city. I don't remember the name of my teacher, only that she had a stiffness to her face and her body that reminded me of the thin-spirited barber who took pleasure in squeezing the backs of our necks way too hard as he trimmed our sparse hair. I hated her and the smell of the room where I took the lessons. I struggled more or less heroically with the piano for a year, before my parents finally relented. I got a little beyond "Long, Long Ago," I think, but not far. Today I don't remember a single line of her music.

The Business of Childhood

ONE TRANSPARENTLY BRIGHT Saturday morning just before I was born, my mother was in our driveway holding onto the handlebars of the thick red "Huffy" bicycle where my oldest brother was sitting skeptically and enthusiastically. A man got out of a car and started walking towards us. My brother looked up at my mother and said, "Who is that man, Mommy?" She said "That's your *father*, honey."

He was just coming back from another week of living in New York City where his job resided. My brother's comment was the last straw. By the time I was born later that year, he had started his own business to which he commuted by walking across the street to the old blacksmith shop that had been in our family for years.

This cedar-sided building with its steep-pitched black roof and rustic doors and windows had seen many lives already. It took on an interesting outward demeanor when my great grandmother, in her seventies at the time, kept a mail-order gift shop there. She had a little wood stove up in the attic which she stuffed full of paper all summer and lit off when the first chill came. This recipe, with a little subtlety added by the fire department, was just the thing to give the outside of the building its unusual black-tinged, severely-weathered look, which has since become a photographer's delight.

Now my father was starting a stitching business that would make the ghostly nylon covers that fit over those steam machines that dry-clean your clothes. (He had designed some of these machines himself.) This new enterprise would employ local stitchers for decades to come. It also employed a family of five kids who rang up hundreds of hours on the time clock at twenty-five to fifty cents an hour.

A long cutting table with a brown masonite top filled one room. A fabric spreading machine and some dangerous electric cutting knives sat on top of it. In another room (where the blacksmith forges still stood in the corners) were five rows of sewing machines with bins of overflowing cloth between them.

When our childhood dies, do ghosts of ourselves stay behind somewhere, perhaps in their favorite haunts? If they do, then there is a ghost of me standing at the end of one particular sewing machine, where Louise Marshall sat for many years. I am telling her a story. I'm such a painfully shy kid that I usually don't open up to anyone. But Louise is the most agreeable person I have ever known. I use her to unleash some of the startling verbal energy that builds up inside me for days. Stories pour out with no editing or proofreading whatsoever, and every half minute or so Louise throws out a random word that gets taken up as raw material into the story, sometimes changing the direction radically. This goes on for hours and she never seems to get tired of it. Does it help her through the long days, or is she just being kind to me?

We kids do a little of everything. We push the fabric spreader up and down the cutting table. We sit at the heavy cast-iron grommet machine and watch our fingers warily as we try to build up speed without getting mangled. When we are not working, we are wheeling each other around on one of the many dolly carts for moving fabric and boxes. Over the years we log thousands of miles on these carts.

But the happiest job by far is helping to "take the dump." Once a week, we slide the heavy cardboard barrels full of fabric scraps onto the dollies and take them to the truck. There are always a few dozen long gray tubes, cardboard cores from the fat rolls of fabric. These are about five or six feet long, very strong and just the right diameter to get a good grip on with two hands. So naturally, we recycle these into hyperactive aggression-release applications, also known as "tube fights." These tube fights have become a tradition by the time my next oldest brother Ted and I get to be the ones "taking the dump."

We put barrels full of tubes outside the shop door. We choose weapons, each trying to find a tube that will hold up longer than the other guy's. We start swinging, pulling them far back over the shoulder and timing ourselves to whack each other's tube with as much force as possible. It makes a loud hollow crack and sends a shock to the wrists. We swing again and again until one person's tube finally breaks and hangs by a shred of cardboard.

When we've demolished all the tubes, which can take us as long as an hour, my father comes out and we ride with him to the dump where we empty the barrels and chuck the limp tubes like javelins into the landfill. We leap back onto the front seat of the truck and ride home in a rumpus of talk and whistling and singing. At the shop we pull in the barrels and put them in their places. We go to the time clock and punch out. It's time to go home.

Finishing the Dictaphone

SHUT UP! THESE TWO MOLEHILL words can quickly grow
mountainous, especially in the mouth of a twelve year old
boy taking the risk of pitching them at his own mother,
more especially when she is standing at the chalkboard in
the kitchen keeping a tally. Every time he says shut up, a
white streak goes up that indicates another ten cents. It's
already up to fifty cents. That boy would do well to shut up
himself, but he is not going to. He's not seeing clearly
where this will end. He's had a bad day today, and he's
throwing his entire capital, of money and parental toler-
ance both, into one crackpot venture. Another white streak
appears. *Shut Up!* he cries.

Supper tonight was one of the worst. Liver again, and
can you believe, lima beans too, all in the same meal? We
ate at the kitchen table, under the big round clock and the
pegboard full of the colored pegs that indicate our chores. I
looked up and remembered that mine included "Put out
milk bottles." I couldn't wait to do that.

My father wasn't home for dinner, and everyone but Ted
and I had managed to get through the liver quagmire and
move on. He and I sat there with nine more bites to take.
And ten of lima beans. My mother had a quirky fondness
for liver. She just couldn't conceive that it belonged in a
special category of its own. We had to take our quota of
bites no matter what.

We asked for the mustard. We shrouded our pieces of
liver, hoping to bury the taste alive. We took a look at each
other, then pinched our noses tightly and picked up our

forks. By closing off the air to your nose, and activating the part of your imagination that tells you you are only eating a piece of ice, you can work miracles. *One-two-three*, I counted. Time was passing. Lima beans, *one-two-three-four*. Gawd. Swallow another glass of milk quick.

My mother got the last bottle of milk from the refrigerator. She set the heavy glass jug in the middle of the table and Ted picked it up and shook it like it was a juvenile delinquent. He poured himself another glass, and so did I. *Four-five-six*. You're getting there. *Five on the beans I think. Five-six-seven…* Time ticked.

Ted and I got through both the liver and the lima beans before our imaginations were sapped. We also polished off the last bottle of milk. Ted had to clear the cluttered table while I went out to the cold entry passage to retrieve the metal rack that held milk bottles. I put six clean bottles in the rack and took them back out. I went to the pegboard, pulled a red peg from next to my name and put it under "Put out milk bottles" next to "Wednesday." In the time it took me to do this Ted had caused everything but the table itself to vanish and had already cleared out. He could be amazing.

"I want you to clean your room before you do another thing, please," my mother said, completely out of the blue. "But I want to work on my dictaphone," I said, referring to a project I had going that employed a crank on a tinfoil wrapped tube and a player arm that held a sewing needle.

"Pick up first, please," she said. It was just then that a number of brightly colored wires that had earlier broken free of the right connections in my brain mingled together like prisoners in a prison yard who were supposed to be exercising instead of talking to each other. It wasn't my mother's orders that got me. It was the whole discouraging day, including the liver and the lima beans.

"*Shut up,*" I whispered softly under my breath.

"*What* did you say?" She looked at me.

"I said, *Shut up!*" It was then that she took chalk in hand and coolly explained the rules of engagement. Ten cents for every time I said it.

Shut Up, Shut Up, Shut Up, I said. Three streaks and thirty cents. "This will come out of your own checkbook," she said, talking about the checking system in which Mom and Dad were the bank, although we used authentic checkbooks to keep track of our savings. "You can write me a check today."

Shut Up. Another streak. *Shut Up.* Streak. *Shut Up!* Streak. That boy went on and on until the blackboard was beginning to look like a picket fence. The mother showed no sign of sympathy and the boy's voice began to take on a disheartened tone. At long last he began to see a real picture in his mind of the ledger side of his checkbook and the big black bottom line that said $5.00. Suddenly his brain was working like the Eniac Computer. He left the kitchen quickly, went to his room and started picking up clothes. When he came across the checkbook with the dark green cover, he stopped and made an entry that all but scoured it clean, then filled out a check which he ripped out and set next to the dictaphone. *Pay to the order of Mom,* it said.

Pete's Assistant

WHEN I WAS TWO, MY FAVORITE pillow was also a notorious cat chaser. She was a boxer named Dinah. As soon as she settled her sleek brown body on the bare floor or on the couch I lay down with my head on top of her and napped or daydreamed until she found something else to do. Dinah was one of the fastest runners on dry land. She could spot a cat as far up the road as you could shout, and get there before it could run up a tree.

In those days, people were not in the habit of keeping dogs confined. Dinah loved to go down the road to harass Albert Knudsen's cows. Mr. Knudsen claimed it got the cows so annoyed they wouldn't give milk. He complained bitterly. My parents tried to keep Dinah on a rope, but she barked so long and loud they had to let her free again.

She also loved to chase Carl Clifford's cats. Carl made his way up the hill to our house once or twice a week to chastise us. It was one time when my father asked *which* of Carl's cats Dinah was chasing that he found out Carl had thirty cats. It was no wonder we'd see a dozen of them at a time on dark nights under the one streetlight on that road, popping up and down like popcorn trying to catch the moths.

My father tried tirelessly to cure Dinah of chasing everything that went on four legs. He even wrote away to a "specialist." He got back a letter dated July 1, 1953. It was typed on a letterhead that read across the top: RICKARD'S ANIMAL MUSK CURE BEATS A BEATING FOR BREAKING DOGS FROM CHASING DEER, RABBIT, FOX, COYOTE, SKUNK. Under that, in very large letters it said PETE RICKARD - Pioneer and Specialist on Animal Scent Glands - Cobbleskill, New York.

> *Dear Mr. Hall,*
>
> *Pete has just given me the answer to your problem which is as follows:*
>
> *He said the glands from just a few cats would not be enough material to make up a musk that would be effective to really break your dog. As a second best method if you really want to break the dog he suggests you make a cage with a wire bottom in it and sit it on top of a cage where your dog can be confined. In the top cage put a cat and keep it there directly over the dog and let the cat urinate over the dog for several days.*
>
> *This method has been used in many cases with best of results altho we admit it is not desirable. But it will break the dog if used long enough because the dog is bound to get sick of cat odor.*
>
> *Thanking you for writing I remain,*
>
> > *Sincerely yours,*
> > "PETE'S ASSISTANT"

My father couldn't bring himself to try this cure in spite of the fine intentions of Pete's assistant. My mother and father realized they were losing all their friends and had to do something about Dinah. They gave her to an uncle. It was a sad day when he came to pick her up and I lost my pillow forever. But she lived happily with him for many years.

Later, the tradition continued with Dinah II, a beautiful purebred boxer who was gentle and never chased a thing. She liked to curl up on my parents' big double bed with my sister's black rabbit. Dinah II was a wonderful dog. She brought us all joy until we found out she had cancer, and another sad day came home to us.

Finally, we had Dinah III. By this time the cars thought themselves more important than creatures who wanted to be free, and we had to build a fence around our yard. This Dinah became my father's dog. She was very gentle too, but loved to play. At about three years old she went completely blind. From then on my father and Dinah were inseparable. "I'm her seeing eye man," he told us.

Dinah III was legendary among local school children who came for tours of my father's factory but spent most of the time out in the field where my father and Dinah demonstrated how they got the better of her blindness. He threw a tennis ball and she ran straight out trying to hear where it fell in the grass. Then she zigzagged back and forth downwind from it until she located it. She never failed the test. My father also made a "buzz bone" for throwing in the water. He put a battery and a buzzer inside a piece of plastic pipe. He switched it on, screwed the cap on and threw it out for Dinah to retrieve. When Dinah got older and lost the use of her back legs, my father made a dolly cart for her, so she could still walk. Finally she got so bad that he knew she had to be put to sleep.

It was not much later that we woke up from these decades of happiness to learn that my father himself was gone. He had used up his heart before he was sixty-six. There hasn't been another Dinah since he died.

Credat Emptor

THERE IS A CURIOUS BUILDING whose main function seems to be to let the traveller know he is at the heart of this little town. A sign out front says *Village Store*, the role it has played since before I was born, but with an uneven career. Its own Platonic script says it is to be dressed in immaculate white clapboards with sparkling windows and six Greek pillars reaching from the ground to the second story across the front.

But it has forgotten its part almost as often as it has strutted its stuff on our stage. The columns were lost before my time. Today it looks joyless. Windows are cracked. Its white clothes have been stripped from it, leaving it half naked through the seasons. It is surrounded by litter. If this is the heart of our town, the passerby might wonder if our heart is broken. It is waiting quietly for its next resurrection.

The enormous granite slabs and stones that support three grand stories actually span a brook that surges beneath the floors. We used to play in this mysterious, stony, watery maze when my father's business, Hall Manufacturing Company, was upstairs. The brook was called Hall's Brook and the store had huge block letters on the facade that said HALL'S, because it was owned by Alpha Hall. I felt we must have a very important name indeed. It didn't matter that the downstairs Halls were no relation to us and that the brook too was probably named for them, not us.

In one of its more memorable roles many years earlier, the store bragged barrels full of molasses and pickles and flour and beans and nails. It sold shoes and buttons and cloth. It delivered goods to the townfolk in a horse and buggy and a little later by a Model T Ford driven by Forace, Alpha's father. A woodstove plucked simple men out of the snow-slow roads to come and talk politics and tell stories.

By the time I got to be the child begging his mother for a penny holiday, Alpha was behind the meat counter, grinding hamburg that would cost us forty-three cents a pound and block-cut chuck roast for forty-one cents a pound. On the front were two round red and white signs that said "Red and White." There was no more Model T, but my mother seldom went to the store except for recreation or effect. Instead, she picked up the black telephone and announced, "*Six-seven-eight*, please."

She dictated her order to "Alphy," who wrote it down carefully on a brown paper bag. As soon as he had time, he went along the shelves and packed our goods into boxes. I would look out the window for his truck, and run to help when he pulled into the driveway. My mother called in almost daily, and, if necessary, more than once a day. This came in handy one year when our household was quarantined for scarlet fever.

Just a dogtrot down Main Street was another store, the "Clover Farm" store owned by Eddie Whitcomb. It was attached to the tiny post office where Postmaster Rodney Wright slapped your mail on the counter with a gentle grin, where Nason Fessenden started his daily journey to take the mail to the mail boxes. My mother tried to support this store too, but it was not quite as convenient, being one block further. They sold home-baked beans on the weekends, probably to try to draw off some business from the other end of Main Street.

Both these stores were gathering places, along with Lawrence Corey's "Old Railroad Snack Bar," homes beyond home for anyone who wanted to be a member of the functional family that was the town. They were institutions that distinguished themselves by their creaking wood floors and warmhearted managers and customers. It gave one a reassuring feeling to open the front door and walk in.

As a reward for being her children, my mother once a week let us select *any* box of cookies we wanted from a short-list of the candidates that won in her pre-election. I loved this time. I usually took a box of animal crackers, even when I knew I should be embarrassed. Sometimes I went for the Cadillac, the tall box of vanilla wafers with the *tromp-l'oeil* image of cookies on the front of the box. I'd grab a stack of these wafers on Saturday morning, to swallow while we loaded glass bottles onto my brother's soapbox-derby cart. We pulled the clanking bottles down the hill to the store and came home brightened with pennies.

Another Saturday I sit in the kitchen pasting Everedy Green Stamps. The books grow pregnant with them, but not quite enough to give birth to a shiny new toaster or coffee machine. Alphy arrives and I stop to help him. I take the nonperishable items to a wide shelf at the top of the cellar stairs. We keep this shelf very well stocked, because the food can be carried down hastily into the cellar to the temporary fallout shelter in case of nuclear attack. A handy first-aid kit with step-by-step printed instructions for nuclear emergencies and extra bandages and aspirin to treat radiation victims is already in the cellar.

The Whistle Bird

I WAS LUCKY TO HAVE A father who spent his life whistling. Ironically, during a childhood when the world huddled nervously beneath a thundercloud of nuclear politics, there was a strange calmness to everyday life. It was common to hear a man whistle while he worked. Where we lived, it was common to hear the birds teaching us how to whistle every morning. In the lofty maple trees and the thick cedar hedge that wrapped around the front of our old New England farmhouse, the birds gathered in pick-up choirs. Nothing could quell their riots. They looted the sunlight's gold and alchemized it into song.

My father must have learned to whistle from these birds, and from Danny Kaye and Bing Crosby. If you found yourself near my father while he was working or playing, you soon brushed against his whistling and it was as good as going to a movie. He had a way of thrusting perfect melodies through his pursed lips like air through a flute. Snatches of song wiffed together with trills and warbles that made one look to see if the windows were open.

Perhaps it was his desire to be like a bird that led him to play dozens of instruments. He was especially fond of the instruments that draw their life from air. He lingered with his clarinet and loitered with the saxophone. He tinkered with penny whistles and recorders and harmonicas. He set the organ stops to every wind instrument it could mimic. He even had a whole set of ocarinas (the smallest one would fit in the palm of one hand, the largest took two arms to hold).

But whistling allowed him to take music with him all day long, and it let him converse with the birds. He seemed to acquiesce in much of the philosophy of a mockingbird that came often to a tree in front of the house across the street from us. My father and the mockingbird could keep it up as long as each had time to waste. The mockingbird's song was loud and rapid as he tried to get a female with as much spring in her as he had. He got my father instead, until at last the bird caught on to the deception. First one would do the mimicking and then the other, and between them they sounded like twenty other birds of the neighborhood. They varied their pitch or their rhythm or their tempo, sometimes interspersing a grating hiss. My father taught the mockingbird a few original pieces as well.

Once walking in the woods in search of Great Blue Herons on a sunny spring day, my father and I saw the fiery orange belly and black and white wings of a Baltimore Oriole flash through the trees, and an instant later heard his song from a nearby thicket. My father imitated this song exactly, and we crept up closer and closer to the bird until we were less than ten feet from his tree, the Oriole singing and peering straight at us, apparently mesmerized by my father's perfect whistle. Their flute-like pipings vibrated skyward through the sunlit pines. The Oriole seemed inclined to stay as long as we would. The song made together by these gleeful virtuosos is still sailing softly in my memory.

My father's birdsong was so convincing that he once was able to trick our most famous local naturalist. On a spring canoe trip the venerable Jeff Smith was paddling in the canoe ahead of my father's canoe. My father craftily whistled the tune of a rare bird. Jeff was so excited to hear it, he stood up to exclaim and point to the woods, and fell over into the river with all his clothes on. This was worrisome because he was 75 years old at the time. They hurried him home and dressed and warmed him, and he was fine. He thanked my father later for the opportunity to hear that bird.

One summer night my brothers and I stood with my father in our front yard inside the cedar hedge. We listened to a vociferous *WHIP-poor-WEEL, WHIP-poor-WEEL* arriving at our ears in endless succession from the dark, a sound mysteriously comforting to childhood. My father started his very loud, perfect imitation and the call came closer and closer through the night. There was a sudden deep whir of wings, as the Whippoorwill dove like a Nighthawk at our heads. We caught the ruby red glare of two small eyes reflected in the light coming from our porch, and the wings seemed to beat right in our ears before they turned up sharply and zoomed into the night sky again. We boys ran screaming into the house.

There is a sound that arrives like an old friend on late winter, early spring days. It is the sound of the Chickadee, not just talking to himself now, *chick-a-dee-dee-dee*, but singing out loud and clear for a mate: *fee-bee,* sometimes *fee-bee-bee,* the second note almost a whole note lower than the first. My father loved to engage the gullible Chickadees. His perfectly pitched imitation convinced even the tiniest of birds, as well it should. It was the whistle of life, and today it still whistles. *Fee-bee, fee-bee-bee.*

Charlotte

I WAS RUNNING TO CATCH UP to my look-alike friend, Peter. We were on our way home from school on a sunny afternoon.

"You wanna come over and finish the game?" I shouted.

"I'd better hoof it home and ask the old lady first," he answered. He was fond of slang. "Should be back in about ten."

A frail figure in a thin brown coat turned the corner at the store behind me. Her hair was put up in a net. She was carrying three books under her arm. As she walked up to me, her jaw began to shake and her teeth began to clatter.

"You get on home now and change your clothes," she said in a watery voice. She pulled in at the Shedd's house and I kept walking.

By the time Peter arrived, my brother Ted was ostentatiously polishing his red hotels on Boardwalk and Park Place, while I was absentmindedly lining up the purple bars of my title deeds to Baltic and Mediterranean, and looking wistfully through a gathering of yellow hundreds hoping to find a five-hundred. The dice were just falling out of Peter's hand when we heard the kitchen door open.

Charlotte put her books on the counter and came into the room where we were on the floor. "Why aren't you boys playing outside on a beautiful day like this?" she said, her loose dentures clattering between every word. "When I was your age, we *never* played inside." She would say the same thing in the middle of a nor'easter or a hurricane. We knew it was coming, but still, the saying of it gave us a new perspective and we hurried to put on our coats and run outside. It *was* a beautiful day.

Charlotte Wright lived two telephone poles up on the other side of the street. She was the town librarian, and easily the best walker in town. On her way to and from the library (that occupied a room in the town hall) she traveled about in her thin-soled shoes, visiting practically everyone, trading information, stories and mail. She was the hardest working of any reporter without a newspaper.

The library was open only from 2 to 4 PM on Tuesday and 2:30 to 4 PM on Saturday, but it seemed to us to be open all the time because Charlotte could always be found. She never levied fines. She knew what everyone was reading and, as she paid her visits, she picked up the books that were due and delivered the books she thought people ought to read.

I was filled with awe on Tuesday and Saturday afternoons when I walked into the high-ceilinged room in the town hall where the aisles were cramped and the books reached all the way to the lights. Charlotte was almost hidden behind the huge counter where I had to stand on a stool to check out books. I couldn't conceive that there were that many books in the world.

If a day started spending itself without Charlotte stopping to visit, my mother got very concerned. Charlotte was part of our family. If there were unwashed dishes in our kitchen, Charlotte washed them. She monitored the laundry, folded the dry clothes and put them away. Charlotte watched us at home and knew everything about us when we weren't home. When my mother wanted to go out and needed Charlotte, she hung a white towel in the front hall window, where Charlotte could see it from her house. She must have looked for it constantly, because she always arrived within minutes.

Her husband suffered from a disease that made him invisible. He seldom left home. I don't believe I ever saw him. I don't think he or Charlotte ate well, because she was as skinny as a penny. On the few occasions one of us went to her house, she would always meet us at the door or come outside. Only my father was admitted to the inside.

Charlotte usually had our mail under her arm when she arrived. She put on her glasses and then handed my father or mother the pieces of mail one at a time. "This is a check from Hoffman Company," she would say, through the continuous racket of her teeth. "This is a bill from Grover Farwell. I should *say*, it's about time. This is an ad. Do you want me to throw it in the wastebasket?"

She got us up to the hour on everyone's life. Even though she knew virtually every secret, her gossip was always sympathetic. She lingered at our house, and next door at Gram Perin's, before she went home. It was common then to be able to drop into houses unannounced. Almost everybody did it. It worked best for Charlotte, since she had neither car nor telephone. She did love to go for a ride with my mother, and would sit waiting patiently in the car for any length of time if she had to.

One day Charlotte came into our kitchen with concern pressed into the many wrinkles of her thin face. She took my mother's hand and guided it to a lump in her side that was the size of an egg. My mother dropped everything and rushed her to the hospital, leaving us home alone. Charlotte never came back again.

Boys and Bees

A MINUTE BEFORE NOONTIME ON a blinding bright June day, a small wasp backed its black and yellow abdomen out of a scarred hole left behind by a maple syrup spigot in a sugar maple tree, pushing with its back legs, then its middle legs and then its front legs until its compound eyes registered a thousand images that came together into tree and field and house. In a confusion of daylight, it spread its front wings and then its hind wings and flew toward a mound of lumber in the middle of the field. In its solitary flight it curved recklessly toward the house, then toward the woods, and finally straightened into a small opening in the stack of wood where it became a social being once again.

His society whirred and hummed in the rotting portion down in the middle of these old planed boards, once neatly stacked in one direction with a few cross pieces, now jumbled and twisted, bleached white in the sun, weathered for half a generation, stroked with heavy black checks and warped up sharply at the ends. As the summer wore on, the city of yellow jackets grew exponentially, although there was no one to witness their frequent coming and going. There was only the small field of overgrown grass and weeds behind a cedar-shingled house that had been abandoned for years. The shingles were weathered gray and black. Only the frames around the four dark windows on the back of the house still held a few clinging flakes of white paint. There was an odd dormer in the roof that could have been designed for dwarves, with tiny black windows. A piece of shingle came loose from the side of the house and flew halfway to the pile of lumber. The towering pines around the edges of the field swayed magnificently.

The yellow jacket was emerging again, its antennae feeling the air and its mandibles pulling at a speck of weathered wood, when it became aware of three giants approaching from the woods. They pounded the earth fearlessly. Boys. They were striding toward the lumber, thinking about Shakespearean stages, riverboats, forts, anything that could be imagined out of an old pile of boards and turned toward an adventure. The yellow jacket pulled in his antennae and rejoined his comrades.

One of these boys was my brother, Ted. One was my friend, Peter Crowell, and the third was me. We had come because this was forbidden territory. The old cedar-shingled building, not far from Peter's house, was one of the two haunted houses in our end of town. It was full of ghosts and possibly a grumpy old man with a gun, though no one had ever seen this man. We hovered near the house as close as we dared, knowing that we would have to be satisfied instead with the pile of lumber. It was close enough to be a dangerously reckless place to play, but far enough to give us half a chance.

As soon as we jumped the pile and Peter started kicking at a board we knew something was wrong. There was a humming and buzzing sound beneath our feet, like thousands of tiny sewing machines working faster and faster. We could almost feel the boards lift, as swarms of black and yellow bodies emerged from the gaps. The noise was deafening. Only Peter had sense enough to turn tail and sprint. He'd already been stung four or five times by then, and a few bees trailed after him as he ran but they couldn't nail him.

My brother Ted and I didn't show the same good sense. In fact, we panicked. We stood flapping our arms, hooting and screaming, stamping on the boards, slapping our thighs and knees and shoulders and brushing at our arms and legs furiously while the bees piled up inside our shirts and pants and stung us from our crew-cut heads to our thin-socked ankles. By the time we started flying, there wasn't a place on our bodies that wasn't pumped full of venom. We ran toward the woods, screaming to the pines, full of fear and poison, and trailed by the last angry wasps. We nearly fell into a cellar hole lined with round stones as we tried to reach Peter's house.

The three of us banged, howling and sweating and squealing, into Peter's kitchen, where we met his mother's surprised face. She located three sticks of butter and smeared us from top to bottom. The bumps on our bodies seemed to sizzle like sautéing mushrooms, and the hundreds of pricks of pain felt sharper and more poisonous the more she rubbed.

To keep from passing out we lay down with our feet propped up. Finally, Peter's mother let my brother and me hobble home. We veered recklessly down the road, unable to walk a straight line. My mother took us to the doctor. We endured a few home days filled with empty nursing before we came back to life. When I emerged again for the first time, it was a magnificent Saturday. The tall pines swayed gracefully as I stopped to sample a breeze blowing from the open field behind our house.

The Devil and Daniel Weaver

I WALKED INTO MY CLOSET AND twisted in the light bulb so I could see. I took down a blue sport coat that had passed through three older brothers into my dark wardrobe. I pulled down a worn white shirt, a red tie and a pair of pants. Under my foot a pine board snapped down and popped up again as I turned to leave the closet. Beneath that board I shared little secrets with the mice that inhabited our walls and floors.

I stood looking into a full length mirror in our huge upstairs bathroom. A family of six other churchgoers milled around me in a cloud of steam and hair tonic. I pulled the fat end of my tie below my belt, and then inched it a bit lower for good measure. I crossed that twice over the narrow end, pinched, pulled it along my neck and down through the loop where it came out too long. I polished my shoes on a cone-shaped buffing pad attached to an electric motor, a machine that had delighted me through most of the 1950's right on into the 60's.

We filed into our customary pew, all but my father and Tom, who were singing in the choir. I sat between Ted and my mother. "Why do they call these pews," I leaned and whispered secretly to my brother, "when it says 'Church Seat' on the bottom of our toilet seat?" I relied on him to catch the irony involved in the word "pew." He seemed to get it.

During the Lord's Prayer by mother's voice echoed through the church, always one embarrassing syllable behind the rest of the congregation. "Our Father, *-ther,* who

art in heaven, -*ven,* hallowed be thy name, -*ame.*" Ted and
I exchanged the usual look. Then the soft fingers of Charlotte Farwell boomed the first line of a hymn on the organ
and we all rose to sing. Our church never had enough
money to install an organ that would play up to tempo.
The Christian Soldiers moved onward, but it seemed they
had to be prodded from behind to make them go. My
mother's syllables continued to echo, this time with the
added embarrassment of pitch darkness. Ted and I smiled
at each other again.

My brother Tom arrived at the end of the pew in his
white robe, carrying the contribution plate. My mother
gave me a tiny envelope with something soft inside it and I
tossed it into the plate. Then the Reverend Daniel Weaver
began his sermon; apparently about money. To me it
seemed odd to be talking about money. Money was just a
part of existence, like sunlight or rain. Sometimes you had
enough of it and sometimes you didn't. It was something
that fell to my grandparents from heaven at Christmas and
on birthdays, though my parents had to search for it every
day in envelopes that my mother opened in the office at
their business, while my father was running relentlessly
around the other rooms.

The meek shall inherit the earth, said Mr. Weaver, but I
was thinking about the stories my father had told me about
one John Elliot, who smelled and looked so terrible when
he came to church suppers, where he always ate like he had
never eaten before. In earlier times, he delivered ice to
houses in Brookline. Once he had blocked the wheels to
his old Ford truck on the steep part of Meeting House Hill
with two chunks of ice while he went into a house to visit.
It was a warm day and when he came out again, his truck
had left him.

One time my father heard the roaring of an engine and a gnashing of mud in our driveway, that repeated itself over and over again. Finally he went out and found John Elliot looking puzzled in the driver's seat of his junk of a truck that was held together with rope and bailing wire. Every time John tried to back up, the right rear fender slid under the wheel and there was an orgy of skidding. My father lifted up the fender with two fingers and said, "Go ahead John," and John backed out while my father walked alongside.

Ye have the poor always with you, but me ye have not always, quoted the minister. But I was thinking that when we got home we would have to take out the garbage to Si Wheeler who would take it home to his pigs. He always scared me, with his white hair, his florid face and bulbous nose and the awful white foam that came from his mouth when he tried to talk. His wife Martha had buried her amputated leg with a full funeral service before she rejoined it. One year she found a silver spoon (once a wedding gift) in our garbage, and came all the way across town to return it.

It is easier for a camel to go through the eye of a needle than for a rich man to enter the kingdom of God, said Daniel Weaver. This image got my attention, and bewitched me. What a thing to say! For all I knew it was just more hocus-pocus. But someone who helped out with writing that Bible sure had a way with words. At the end of the service I shook the minister's hand and said "Good morning" bravely as we filed past him out of the church.

Sound Effects Men

I F YOU WERE LYING ON YOUR stomach on the metal floor of a small private plane flying low over our little town, with your head sticking out the door, looking straight down, and your feet hooked onto a seat, you would see what looks like an ocean of green virgin forest, with two white steeples emerging from the top of it, and a few buildings and roads nestled into the hills, along with some ponds and rivers. In the middle of things, where three roads converge, you would see a tall, square yellow building with a handsome roof.

If you were a tourist driving through the village center in a rented Subaru with your wife in the passenger seat, you would probably stop in front of the yellow building and get out to snap a picture of it, after setting the camera lens to a wide angle. You would read the large black letters that say *Daniels Academy Building* across the front of the handsome yellow building with white columns, and as you got back into your Subaru, you would look around for the students eating lunch on the grass and chatting with a bald professor with a mustache and sunglasses. But you wouldn't see anyone there, except a member of the town's conservation commission coming out of the big front door and pulling annoyingly on his gray beard, with a vacant expression on his face.

Daniels Academy Building is no academy, but our town hall, large enough, when I was little, to hold practically the whole population. One wealthy Mr. Daniels had left a sum to be put aside for a hundred years until it would be worth millions, and could build a great academy in our midst.

Townfolk couldn't wait that long, and they needed a meeting place, so they broke the will and built a town hall that would look more at home in a small city. They named it Daniels Academy, to honor Mr. Daniels and his fetching ideas.

I had to go to the town hall recently to register my car and my dog. Before I left, I turned and climbed the unlit front hall stairs, making the wide, varnished maple boards creak, and sliding one hand along the dark banister until I reached the landing. I entered an enormous empty hall where I had spent many hours of my childhood, and I found the place cool and dark and filled to the ceiling with echoes.

There goes one now. The moderator brings the gavel down with a cavernous bang on a wooden table set up on the stage. Citizen A is wiping the steam from his heavy glasses and shouting at citizen B. Why did Mr. B have to dump his load of pig manure so close to where Mr. A is going to be building his new driveway? The voices argufy, and mingle with hoots and laughter. Bang again. "Closing under article six, and opening under article seven."

Men's and women's voices spill from the stage, uttering lines from *Arsenic and Old Lace,* mixed confusingly with pieces of other plays. The soft sound of tickets dropping into penny raffle cans trips from the walls. David Shedd's young voice, making itself husky and convincing as a cobbler, steps down from the stage dressed in a tiny cloud of jealousy. My father and my brother are singing "Barnacle Bill the Sailor," and there are shrieks of laughter racing around me on the floor.

Another young voice recites "The Wreck of the Hesperus," and an echo that seems to arise outside and inside my head at the same time is carefully retelling "The

Yarn of the Nancy Bell." Mrs. Varney's steel voice announces winners of the prize speaking contest. There is the sound of a movie projector, a dance band, a player piano, a hundred instruments, not playing in time, but playing time itself.

In a corner backstage hangs a twenty-foot-high sheet of metal. This was the "thunder sheet" my father labored so hard to forge for *Blithe Spirit*. If I rattled it now, the town clerk downstairs would go into shock, but I can hear the slow rumble of thunder coming in from far away and getting louder. My father not only could build thunder sheets, he could act the thunder convincingly, because he practiced it as much as his spoken lines. He prided himself on being able to imitate almost any sound, by mouth, by hands, by instruments, by machinery. For months he filled the rooms of our house, far and near, with the bloodcurdling wail of a ghost. I hear it again now, rising in an unearthly crescendo from backstage.

That play also needed a rain machine, so my father applied his engineering background to the job. He drilled a hole in the center of the bottom of a round cake tin, mounted it on the spindle of an old turntable and filled the tin with BB shot. He put this rain machine backstage with a microphone close to it. When the BB's rolled around in the tin and the noise was amplified, it came out sounding just like rain, and people in the hall marveled.

The voices and the echoes in this room are beginning to encourage each other. I need to leave. There is work to do. I head for the bottom floor and earth. The voices want to follow, but I close the door on them and keep on going.

Fire in the Pine Grove

M Y FRIEND PETER CROWELL was a source of secret information that was as reliable as our electricity in a thunderstorm. One muggy June morning I was casually checking our candle supply, when a knock came on the kitchen door. It was Peter. Did I want to come out and ride bikes? O.K.

"Your brother Ted and Bruce Jones and them — all smoke ciggies up in the pine grove, you know," Peter pronounced as we pedaled our fat bikes up Old Milford Road.

"They do not," I whined back, singing the "do."

"I'll show you the butts," he said. "Come on."

We turned around and raced down the hill in high gear. In those days, high gear meant you moved your legs very fast, not very slow. I pulled the chain on my silver siren, for good measure, and cats and crows vanished through the trees with fear in their eyes.

We leaned our bikes against the huge sugar maples that stood like sentries on either side of my gravel driveway. We crossed the street without checking for cars, and started up a steep dirt road with a grass hump in the middle of it.

"What will you do for me if I show you the butts?" asked Peter, halting abruptly on his side of the hump.

"Too many ifs, ands and *butts*," I said, feeling clever. "Let's go."

"Would you eat a worm?" he asked decisively.

"You do it," I said bravely.

He searched some mud and pulled up a worm. He turned his profile to me, held the worm like a piece of spaghetti and dangled it slowly into his mouth. He swallowed hard and said, "There." He seemed satisfied that I had paid my price of admission, and we went on.

We were about to reach the site of the Eleusinian Mysteries of Brookline, where my older brother and his friends did things that I could not credit when I heard the report of them, like indulging in relentless supplies of gum and candy, like telling dirty jokes for half-hours on end. As we approached we heard voices. Peter and I looked at each other.

At the edge of the dirt road lay a carpet of poison ivy like a bed of nails. Behind were ferns and sarsaparilla, a few maple saplings and a wild grape vine winding round a dead oak. Further behind was a thicket of young pine trees, thin enough to let tiny circles of light project onto the tips of a few green leaves low to the needled floor, but thick enough to hold down most of the undergrowth. It formed a perfect hiding place for my older brother and his friends, a beautiful temple of counterculture, where mostly shadow prevailed, with a few bars of sunshine lighting the dead arms and fingers of the pines, unsafe ladders to the green summit above.

We sidestepped the poison ivy and entered the secret copse, where my brother Ted and Bruce Jones and two other kids sat and talked. They were surprised, but welcomed us. Peter shrank down by a ring of small stones and took off his shoes. He picked up a cigarette butt from the fire pit and held it up daintily for me to see. Bruce came over and dumped out the contents of a small leather pouch. A pile of butts spilled out, many of them colored with bright pink lipstick. Bruce's parents, Bruce Sr. and Mimi, smoked like two abused and overworked rubber tires, and it was young Bruce's habit to gather up the tiny butts all over his house and bring them to the pine grove where they were good for two or three more puffs.

I was filled with disbelief. It turned to apprehension, as they lit up the fire pit, overloaded with dead branches, leaving the thick smoke to amass and blunder through the canopy above us. Peter danced around the roaring fire, singing *Dirty Li'l, Dirty Li'l, Lives on top of garbage hill, Never washes, Never will, KWIK POO, Dirty Li'l.*" Nothing new from Peter. We all circled around the fire, hacking and spitting into it on *Kwik Poo* .

A heap of brown leaves and dry twigs and branches lay recklessly close to the fire and no one noticed when a spark flew into them. In seconds, the flames rose like devils in front of us and the older boys and I began running around screaming. All of us had bare feet. No one dared jump on the fire and no one had a better plan. We were about to see the whole temple go up and the whole counterculture come down. Just then, a sunbeam struck Peter. He let out a war whoop and hurdled into the flames in his bare feet. He kept bouncing and shrieking, raising his knees up to his neck, while the rest of us looked on. He overwhelmed the fire and let out another whoop. We all took a deep breath.

When the group had finished congratulating itself, Peter and I hurried back down the hill. He grabbed his bike to head up the road and I pushed mine into our barn. *Dirty Li'l, Dirty Li'l,* I heard him singing softly to himself as he pedaled home.

Family Trees

GRAM PERIN SAT WITH HER feet tucked up to her chin in the seat made by the big branches of the apple tree, in the middle of the yard behind our white clapboard house. It was a hot July day in 1879 and she was reading a book of tales by Hans Christian Anderson. She was 10 years old. A wonderful breeze rushed up the field and over the stone wall and shook the leaves of the apple tree, turning the page for her before she was ready. But she didn't notice, because she fell asleep in the same moment.

When she awoke, another family had moved into the white clapboard house, my family. She had climbed down from her comfortable place and lived her life. She was in her nineties and now she lived in the small white house behind ours that was once the cooper shop. She recited Mother Goose to us and made pull candy, and we played ball in the back yard and read books in the apple tree while she misplaced everything she owned one item at a time, until we found it all for her and she started over again.

By this time the apple tree had the kind of character with which you wanted to be associated. She not only had wonderful arms to climb into, but she was so old and venerable, she was a little fearsome to behold. We climbed all over her anyway. We used her for first base and we gathered up her fallen branches after heavy storms.

Almost every house has its outdoor relatives, its apples or maples or cherries, spruces or oaks – brothers, sisters, uncles, aunts, grandparents, that put down their roots and never walk away. Our house was surrounded by kindred trees, but there were three trees in the back yard that our lives especially were bound to: the apple, the elm and the Weeping Willow.

One year, the apple tree grew too old to keep trying, even with all our care. The sky in our back yard was left with a big hole in it, and first base became a mound of grass. We felt so bad we drove out in our Chevy on Mother's Day and bought a young Weeping Willow to put in a corner of the yard to try to fill the apple tree's shoes. But ants attacked it. It grew at a terrible angle and at a miserable rate year after year, and my father and I tied a rope to it from a pine tree in the woods a hundred feet off, in an effort to make it grow straight. It was always crippled, but we loved its little green tails swinging in the wind, and we talked about it all the time, even after it too became a wispy hole in the sky.

In the other corner stood a gigantic American Elm that grew to a towering height because it was located over the septic tank. One year Gram Perin hired a neighbor to dig a hole for a new septic tank. We knew him well, with his white hair, bulbous nose, faded blue eyes and bib overalls. His name was Arthur Popple, but I called him Martha Popple. He lived with his sister, Mable Popple, and he was slightly retarded. Gram found work for him when she could. He labored behind our house for days digging an enormous hole, but when the state came to inspect it, the state said the hole didn't meet a single regulation and it was unusable. Gram asked Arthur to fill it back in. He broke down and cried. It gave us all a start. Before that we hadn't quite known that he had feelings.

The elm tree caught the Dutch Elm disease about the same time as the elms that lined both sides of Main Street. Since it hung over the stone wall outside our play area, its falling limbs were no danger. So we let the elm slowly die and lose his hair and turn into a skeleton during the whole period of my growing up. We watched the sunset every night through his stately, but shrinking crown. The flames turned the whitened branches into black silhouettes. We photographed it and watched it fall, for decades. It grew more and more beautiful the more closely it embraced the sky.

When one of my brothers got married in our back yard, and he and his fiancée had been unable to decide on music for the wedding, a Baltimore Oriole came to the branches of the elm tree and sang through the entire ceremony. It left when the groom kissed the bride and we marveled as the sunset came again behind the elm and we watched it through the glorious fog of a remarkable punch we had consoled ourselves with. My sister took a picture of the elm with the sky in it, called it "Elegy for an Elm," and won first prize in a contest.

Long after the apple tree and the Weeping Willow tree were gone, the elm was still with us, in his fashion. There was talk of trying to ease his death by killing him more quickly, but everyone knew we wouldn't. He fell piece by piece, as every evening the orange sky turned his grace to glory. The more we watched the wiser we grew. By the time he gave his last bone to the sky, it felt almost like we knew something.

The Bottom of the Dream

I AM FOURTEEN AND I AM dreaming. I move past the little
red door called the "chute" where we throw out our trash,
and I leave the house through the kitchen door. I step over
a milk-bottle basket and a pile of overshoes and enter a five-
story brown wooden maze known as our barn. In Vermont
and Maine they have more "bahs" in their barns. Our barn
has more "are" in it, but not much. It is spelled "bahrn."

As I pass under a sign that says "Beware of the Cat," I
see a streak like a shooting star in the opening left by the
sliding barn door. I hear a whining voice like a baby's, cry-
ing "Lemme-owt! Lemme-owt!" I roll over in my sleep and
push the black cat off my bed.

I heave the big black sliding door all the way open to let
more light into the dream. My brother Ted jumps off the
half-floor twenty feet above my head, swinging through the
middle of the damp air on a thick rope. When he lands on
the barn floor, I lift my foot and pull out a nail that is sticking through it.

I climb some rough-hewn wooden stairs. My mother is
just latching the hand-forged hook in the wooden gate at
the top of the stairs. David Hobart Jr. brings down a heavy
hammer on the anvil of his blacksmith shop across the
street. I turn away my eyes. I lift the hook from its iron seat
and my mother vanishes. I am in the middle of a jungle of
necessary and unnecessary things. There are cedar chests,
and skis and skates, headboards and bedsprings and barn
swallows and a grinding wheel, and chairs, broken and unbroken, a crumbling black baby carriage on huge wheels,

and a leaning cider press. My mother's white rocking horse on runners is rocking beside the red one on springs that I used to use. An old box of jars is spilling onto the floor. When I pick one up, my mother reappears and tells me a story. Those were the jars Gram Perin was told to label "Cold Tomatoes" when she worked in a factory in Boston. Instead she set the stamping machine to say "Old Tomatoes" and she got fired.

When my mother vanishes again, I dare to try the narrow, steep wood stairs to the top floor of the barn, being careful on the fourth step, which has split into a half step and is treacherous. I reach a dizzy height. If I could see through the cloudy row of fourteen lights across the front of the barn, I would be looking down at the bits of sky that ride by on blue jay backs, and on the barn swallows coming and going through the barn door. I push a huge broken hay rake to one side and it swings back to trip me. I land in a pile of small boxes that Gram Perin used in her religious gift shop. I pick up a wooden cross from the floor and thrust it through my brother's heart like a sword. He gives me a big hug.

I hear noises and open my eyes and see a light. My brother Ted is just going to bed in the bed next to mine, but I am already back in another dream. I am in "Grandpa's room," a room built into the back of the other loft of the barn. I pick up a stuffed bird from the floor. I pull a book off the shelf and a flock of books flutters out the window. Outside the room I lift the rusted, curved horn of an old Victrola from the floor of the loft. I put it to my ear and my grandfather hands me a dollar. I nearly step off the edge of the loft where there is no railing. I see some giant stilts leaning below me and climb onto them, walking across the barn floor and out into the driveway where my father looks up at me with a big smile on his sunlit face. "They work pretty good, don't they?" One stilt comes down on a stone and goes out from under me. I float slowly down and find myself on the bottom floor of the barn, down in the root of the dream, down the stairs that go into the remains of a chicken coop and into the cool, damp rooms where horse carriages are parked rotting, full of faded families.

I am about to enter the secret room, the one in the far back through piles of rubble, the one through a secret door set into unfinished boards as broad as a man's shoulders, attached to hand-hewn beams, resting on monolithic cut granite blocks and round boulders. I crawl through into the damp, unlit room and find my brother Ted in there. There are piles of old picture frames everywhere. There's a black and white photo of a painting of a child who is leading a lion and a cow and a lamb and a wolf. Ted hands me a treasure, and it makes me glow like the sun, inside my dream. I don't know what it is.

We are surrounded by hand-cut picture puzzles made by a man Gram Perin hired. Ted opens a door to a strange compartment in the wall, and there is the man, hanging by the neck from a rope, with a bottle in his hand. He looks at me and speaks. "I didn't know," he says. "I didn't know how we need these things. We need these things!" I close the door.

Tuning the Glasses

IT'S TIME TO TALK ABOUT kitchens. Kitchens are the hands of a house, the hustle that shows what a house is made of, the household's grip on life. They are also the face. A home's character shows clearly in the kitchen. If the kitchen's face is lazy, the whole place is probably lazy. If it is too efficient, the whole place is probably too efficient. If it is humorless, most likely the whole house is starved for humor. The kitchen that has just had a makeover can keep up its airs for only so long before the home's true personality bursts again onto the scene.

In those days when we were abandoning telephone operators to the wonder of finger-spun dials, our kitchen was so devoid of airs that it wouldn't have hurt anything if it had taken some on. What it lacked in elegance it made up for in friendliness, and size, and willingness to tolerate a hungry family of seven, and the peculiarities of my father and mother.

It was a big kitchen. A long counter, round at the end, jutted into the middle. Its surface was made of something that looked like blue linoleum, with a wide steel band running around it. On top of it sat a deep-fat fryer, some half-emptied glass milk bottles, a glass bottle of Heinz ketchup, a carton of salt, somebody's jacket, an unopened can of peaches, and an endless onslaught of food passing from the refrigerator to the table on the other side of it, and dirty dishes passing from the table in the well-known direction of the sink.

In later years, when my father bought a new embroidery machine for his sewing factory, he tried it out by stitching some large white letters on a red cloth, and he made a banner that hung on the kitchen wall for years. It said, "It takes a living heap, to make a house a home."

Next to the kitchen door was a small red door my father had built into the wall, with a long chute on the other side that ran down into the big trash barrels out in the barn, which could be switched when they were full. "Put it down the chute," was something I heard often. The "chute" was beloved by family and visitors alike. It was fun, gave us philosophical studies in the problems of materialism and was an emergency access to the house, since you could just reach the lock on the kitchen door by stretching one arm through it.

The kitchen was painted a fiery red up to waist level and light blue above that. The floor was a dark blue, marbly linoleum and the ceiling was white except for the vast, sooty ring beginning above my mother's electric stove, turning to lighter and lighter rings of gray as you got further from the stove. It was a waste of time to either wash or paint this ceiling since my mother had her own ideas about its color scheme.

Near the stove was the communication center of the house, the black telephone, a blackboard covered with phone numbers and a cork board in a gray frame painted with flowers. Beneath the cork board was a small button. For years I was an avid student of drums and spent hours practicing in my room upstairs, very far from the kitchen. No one could call me, short of coming to my room to tap on my shoulder, so my father wired a light bulb to the wall in front of the drums and ran a wire all the way down to the kitchen. They could call me any time by pressing the button. It must have taken a few hundred feet of wire.

Next to this button was a big blue cast iron radiator that kept my mother's bread rising and felt good to sit on while you observed life in the kitchen. Most of this life took place at the long table in the alcove between the radiator and the central counter. This was the scene of thousands of meals, countless raucous planning sessions and dozens of grisly engagements with lima beans and liver.

One year, the table was preoccupied for weeks by my father's obsession with music. He had a huge collection of musical instruments, and played them all, but he had never played the glasses. So he covered the whole kitchen table with wine glasses of all shapes and sizes, filled them with water to different heights and carefully tuned them, using a spoon to hit the sides and to move water from one glass to another.

Eventually he had what he wanted, and after a few days practice he could play beautifully, dipping his fingertips in a separate water bowl and running them around the rims of the glasses. Naturally, he didn't stop until he could get three and even four-part harmonies by using his thumb and little finger on each hand and rearranging the glasses.

By the time the water in the glasses was undrinkable, my father had achieved his goal. We tried it out ourselves too. We listened and made our own harmonies to the best of our ability. Some sounds were worth forgetting and some chords were good enough to vibrate down decades to our own children. Today, we keep trying to be my father's music, but we can't play the whole piece. At least we grew up knowing pretty much what kitchens are for.

Hiding in the Mailbox

O<small>NE YEAR</small> I <small>WAS TRAVELING</small> with a friend on the back roads of Greece, trying to track down the best preserved but most remote Greek temple, which happened to be deep into the rural nub of the Peloponessus. We drove our cloud-gray Opel Kadett station wagon into a tiny town along the road, a town whose name I don't know. I say drove, but we might as well have got out and pushed, because the road was so full of dogs and chickens and goats and cats that you could only move a few feet at a time, honking the horn to clear a path. After the charm wore off, I grew annoyed. But as I slowed down more and more, and began to approach my own thinking speed, an epiphany came to me, just in time. This was the way, I thought to myself, things *should* be.

We never had it quite that good when I was growing up in the 50's and 60's on a quiet road in rural New Hampshire. But we kids and animals still were pretty sure that the road belonged to *us*, and we spent a good deal of our time in the middle of it. Like kids everywhere, we had dozens of ways to use a paved surface. There was the single sturdy red tricycle that turned itself into two small bicycles with training wheels that turned themselves into five bigger bicycles with sirens on them. There was the soapbox derby cart, that turned itself into a way to rattle returnable bottles to the store once a week and make some small change. It later became a motorized go-cart that swerved crazily to the edge of the road to make room for cars. There was the skateboard, and the Vespa scooter that carried it to the top of the hill with a passenger on the back screwing up his courage to make the run.

There was the pogo stick on which I set a new record, something over a thousand jumps. There were the giant stilts you climbed onto on the second story of the barn. There was the little square car called a "King Midget," about twice the size of a golf cart. My father taught us how to drive in "Midgy" on Rocky Pond Road, a dirt road that was pretty much a stranger to cars.

Then there were the things you did without wheels, the games made with a piece of chalk, the hundreds of rolls of caps pounded into the pavement with eroding points of stone, the games of catch and kickball. We loved to stomp puffballs and to string milkweed pods end to end across the street and crouch on the edge of the road waiting patiently for a car to come and pop the pods, and send the seeds blowing to become a new crop.

One year, my mother bought new dishes, something called "Boonetonware" made of a space-age material guaranteed not to break under normal use. We tried dropping them on the floor from various heights and they didn't break. We wanted to try a harder surface, so we took them out into the road and scaled them up and down. They still wouldn't break. Only one bowl ever broke and that was when my mother set it down full of soup, gently, in front of a guest. Then it cracked, not under the pressure of the moment, but as the result of its traumatic childhood.

It seems the cars were better educated back then than cars today. They knew to look for irrational things in the road. At least all but a few of them did. A few were straight-ahead types that repressed the irrational. They would gather speed coming down our long hill and became such a menace to children and animals that my father one year put out a large sign that said, *Danger, Live Children Ahead.*

One time my mother was walking on the sidewalk on Main Street when a truck full of potato chips came careening into town as though it were still on the open road. Bill Shutt, whose house was on Main Street, was so angry he stepped right out into the road in front of the truck. My mother watched, holding her breath, not knowing if Bill Shutt was going to live through it. "There's children around here," Bill shouted when the truck driver jumped out of his truck. It's a good thing there weren't any children there at that moment, when the truck driver began to mention his own views to Bill.

By far, my favorite thing to do on the road was to hide in the large wooden mailbox my father had built to hold packages for his business. It was just big enough for two kids to squeeze in and pull down the canvas cover over the front. One day my friend Peter Crowell and I were sitting in there eating sandwiches when Nason Fessenden pulled up to deliver the mail. We crouched in the back, but I'll never forget the expression on his face when he lifted the canvas to throw in the packages.

For years the cars on our road were generally friendly with each other, stopping often to chat, and friendly with the slower creatures who shared the road with them. But then new cars, as if by magic, began to discover the charms of our rural road, began to think the road belonged to them. They joined others and became a juggernaut of reason. Who can argue? They are driving toward a new century. They know where they are going. Why make a case for the road itself, when the end of the road seems to be in reach?

At the Barbershop

O<small>N THE FIRST DAY OF APRIL</small>, in 1959, my father, a brother and I were sprawled out across a vinyl couch that was the front seat of our green and white Chevy. There would have been room for a football player between each of us. We were driving to the barbershop in the town next to ours. After waving to a few people, we turned into a parking place on the Milford, New Hampshire oval. Across the street was a plate glass window with red and white letters painted onto it and a spinning red, white and blue barber's pole next to it.

I watched as my father leaned forward and turned the key in the ignition. It was peaceful when the car stopped rumbling. He quickly concealed the ring of keys over his window visor, where no one would think to look, and we jumped out of the car into a day full of sunshine.

"She's adorable," he said, looking down at a baby in a stroller that was being pushed by a young woman with red hair. "The baby's pretty cute too," he said matter-of-factly. We didn't laugh.

We followed him between the faded white lines of the cross walk and into the barbershop. I glanced at the spinning barber's pole as we entered. "How *does* that thing go?" I asked my brother Ted.

"Don't ask so many questions," he answered helpfully, "and don't keep your mouth open all the time."

Ted and I sat on metal chairs in the brightly lit room, beneath a long mirror on a white wall. Between us was a little table with metal legs and a yellow top, covered with magazines, *Gun World*, the *Saturday Evening Post*, *Gun Digest*, the *Gun Gazette*.

My father settled into one of the two big barber's chairs that looked to me like dentist chairs. He joked with the barber, who fastened the bib tightly around his neck.

The air was saturated with the smell of hair-tonic escaping from open bottles. The floor was strewn with small piles of hair waiting to be swept behind a heavy curtain left partially open at the back of the room. This curtain always had a gap at the right side, leading into the darkness behind, making you wonder what was back there and what the barber did when he occasionally entered the shadow.

"Are you here to get a haircut?" I asked my brother across the little yellow table, using my politest voice.

"Yes Ma'm," he answered. "How 'bout yourself?"

"Me too. Think of that. Both of us here for the same reason, to get a haircut!"

A man with a bulbous nose and sparse hair who was sitting in the corner glanced up from his newspaper briefly. My father looked in the mirror, ran two fingers over his ear, then got down from the barber chair and thanked the barber. The barber motioned to me to climb up into the chair and I went.

This wasn't the barber who smoked fat, stale cigars and blew the smoke in your face. This was the barber with a crew-cut and military bearing, and bare arms and large hands. He was notorious for the delight he took in squeezing the back of young boys' necks when he wanted them to turn their heads one way or another, or even when the urge just came over him for no reason at all. We hated him and his thumb and third finger, but we were careful to never let out any indication of the pain and fear he generated. My father was paying money for this after all, and the alternative was to suffer the presence of superfluous hair on your head.

He wrapped me in the bib and tightened it snugly around my throat. He pulled out an electric razor that sounded like a model airplane and started shearing the sides of my head like a nurse prepping me for an operation. Then his big hand went around the back of my neck. My neck stiffened like a gun barrel as his fingers dug into it.

"Turn your head you little loser, you big-eared creep with white skin, or I'll cut both ears off with this razor," he said.

I can't say if those were his exact words, but that was the feeling of it, pretty much. I turned my head one way, but he twisted it the other and went back to his shearing.

When he was done with me, he did my brother. My father opened his wallet and handed over a few dollar bills as my brother and I waited at the door. We walked out into the sunshine and I glanced at the spinning barber's pole again. We crossed between the white lines and headed back to our car.

It was still the first of April and it was a beautiful day with a blue sky. The cool air brushed my bare neck and passed its gentle fingers over my ears. The smell of hair tonic floated along with us. We hopped into the Chevy. My father grabbed the keys off the visor. We backed out and rumbled off, just as if we weren't in the middle of a cold war, just as if my father's broad smile and clean face and unpredictable jokes were the only thing that mattered to us.

Maude Luman's Lobster Salad

I HAD TO GET THE BLUE WALLPAPER off the wall by washing it with a sponge soaked in vinegar. I couldn't stop thinking about corned beef and cabbage the whole time. It's not too often in the long life of a New England farmhouse that a boy's bedroom gets new wallpaper. There was good reason to get the last strands of paper off the bumpy plaster wall quickly, and to do it right. Maude Luman was coming.

If you had wallpapering to do in those days (and you lived in our town) you called Maude Luman. When she pulled up in her station wagon you didn't offer to help her carry her ladders and table and buckets, even though she was well into her eighties and barely as tall as her car. That would have been the same as coming right out and saying she shouldn't pick up two ladders, a box of wallpaper, a bucket of tools and a heavy drop cloth all at once. And it would have been asking for a rebuke that would make you feel smaller than she was.

There wasn't a fussier, faster worker, or tougher girl in New England. But wallpapering was only Maude's part-time job. Her full-time job was working in my parents' stitching business, where she tarried for over 20 years. She was almost ninety when her wiry body and white hair and wrinkled face no longer appeared daily at her sewing machine, and that was only because she couldn't see well enough any more to sew.

Maude came to New Hampshire from Nova Scotia, and brought with her such a corpus of independence and hard-headedness that she didn't need to learn anything from the

Granite State. She wouldn't take orders from anyone but herself, and sometimes she wouldn't even take those. She exacted as much from her body as she did from her mind. Old age made her demand even more. My father exclaimed, over and over, "Boy, she's a tough old bird!"

One of her jobs was to stitch zippers onto Bible covers. She prided herself on piling up more every day than the other stitchers. When she was in her mid-eighties she began to worry that she might not keep up. She kept a count in her head. When she had a good day she stashed her extra covers in a hiding place by her feet. She could pull out a few of these when she had a bad day. If she ever came close to going down in defeat, she worked right through her break.

But breaks were usually the time she, more or less unintentionally, kept everyone entertained. While the other stitchers chatted and drank coffee, Maude climbed up onto the big cutting table to do her exercises, bicycle pumps, sit-ups, and so on. It was not unusual to walk into the factory and see her doing a headstand on the cutting table, like an upside down statue of herself. Occasionally she wanted to rest instead of exercise, and then she lay down and snoozed in one of the long cardboard boxes that the rolls of fabric came in. She said she planned to use one of these boxes for her coffin.

She may have owed her long life and health to unrelenting work, and exercise in between, but there was another even more important factor. Garlic. If she felt a cold approaching her, or anything else evil, she ate whole bulbs of raw garlic. She often came to work with garlic cloves hanging on a string around her neck. She'd smell up the whole place with garlic fumes. She prescribed it to the other stitchers, but they got a good dose of it just by being in the same room with secondhand garlic. She had dozens of other home remedies as well, and little patience for those who didn't believe in them.

It was Maude Luman who made church suppers such a success, or at least the ones with lobster salad. Maude drove to the docks in Porstmouth, and bought mountains of used lobster bodies for ten cents a pound. She and ten or twelve other ladies of the church, including my mother, would sit in a circle in the church kitchen and pick out the lobster meat under Maude's direction. Maude tried to prod everyone to be as fast, and fussy, as she was, but she did the bulk of the work herself. She could crack the tiny pincers on the ends of the legs and pluck out every molecule of meat. The others tried and tried, but got giggly and gabby when they couldn't do it. That made Maude mad. She couldn't understand anyone who could let a morsel of meat go on lingering, maybe even go to its grave, in a hard shell.

In her later years, as Maude sat at her sewing machine, and her eyesight was disintegrating, I would sometimes hear a small, sharp yelp come from the part of the room where she was stitching. She would stand up calmly and walk over to my father, who would grab a pair of pliers and pull out a needle that had gone straight through her finger. Maude looked on with small, bright eyes, not saying a word while he pulled. She waited politely while he put a bandaid on her finger. While the rest of us looked on alarmed, she hurried back to her sewing machine, still without a word, sat down, and kept on stitching.

New Hampshire

New Hampshire. Hush. And don't listen. I'm going to talk about you. Embrace Vermont in your modest way. Turn your coy back on Maine. Let Canada cool your head. Keep your foot on Massachusetts. Darken your great smiling faces with squalls. Cover your maternal mountains with bright colors. I'm going to use words that are immodest.

School is out. Four boys and their young sister are packing the covered green truck. The mother is thinking about sandwiches and milk, and the father is thinking about rope and sails. I climb into the wide middle seat, next to a window with a torn "I Like Ike" sticker on it that can be read from the inside but not the outside. Others burst into the rear seat.

We leave the southern part of New Hampshire that is so populated you can buy a washing machine and still do other things in one day, and we rumble toward the place we call simply "the lake," south of the Old Man, south of the pyramid of Chocorua, cooling the feet of the poetic Ossipees, Lake Winnipesaukee, the face of the great smiling spirit, waters on loan from those Indian ghosts that paddle and wait so patiently.

We drive for three hours, and then unload onto the pine-needled ground and into the green cottage of my father's childhood, on Melvin Bay. We peel off our shoes and throw them into a closet, since we won't need them for a time that seems to us like half of the whole year. After the first weekend, my father and my uncle go home to work, while my mother and aunt and nine children settle into the green camp. My grandmother and her sister and their retired husbands are already nestled into the brown camp that rests below the giant pines behind us, further from the water's edge.

"Beauty, truth and rarity, Grace in all simplicity." You need Shakespeare to tell you what you have here. What child knows he was in paradise, without a poet to tell him? Reverie and silence. Pleasure, peace, moisture's potential. The body at its best. Windflaws and whistling of loons. Spray on the face. Blue sky, cumulus clouds. Sunsets that burn inside. Stars that grow a mind. New Hampshire, I told you. Immodest words.

While my blond hair is bleaching white and my skin risks the sun, the loud horn of the mailboat bends the corner into our bay. Twenty children run to be first to the dock. We wave to the passengers as a man lowers the mail in a fishing net from the wooden bow that stops against an invisible bumper hanging from the landing. We sit and divide the mail to a dozen camps, the houses of Merrymount. I am related by blood to some of these families, but I am related by time to all of them. I have many sets of aunts and uncles along this shoreline, and I choose to deliver the mail to a house at the far end where the candy is the best.

Tomorrow I pump out the boats at the dock, I swim for hours and canoe to Store Island. I lie in the sun on the gray dock and I roam the shoreline engaged in imaginary adult vocations and innocent flirtations with my second cousins. I learn some bizarre theories on the facts of life from a clutch of kids gibbering in the boat house where we are not supposed to be. (After a few years these theories turn out to be true.) I play in the sandpile with the smaller kids. My cousin and I lock another cousin into the tiny playhouse and throw stink bombs in with her. I play monopoly in the slanting sunlight of late afternoon and pass more money under the table than on top of it. My father arrives that night and takes us to the movies in Wolfeboro. I ride there with a cute second cousin and torture my brain with how to entertain her with my wit. Finally I sing softly to myself, "You smell too much to be true. Can't keep the flies off of you..." I can't tell in the dark if she is laughing or not.

In the morning we get up early because it is the day to launch Tordzus. (She is named Tordzus because someone said she looked so funny coming *towards us*.) This big gaff-rigged catboat is the oldest sailboat on the lake. It has been in my family since my father was in his twenties. It takes a whole day to launch her from her wooden dolly with no wheels. We carry the planks and heavy pipes from stern to bow, and push until she is in the water. It is an occasion for all of Merrymount. As soon as Tordzus hits the water, she begins to sink. We let her stay under for a week, then tackle her with buckets and the gas pump and spend another whole day stepping her mast and rigging her. I don't know it is happening, but this sailboat is making herself synonymous with childhood, and with the responsibility that lives hand in warm hand with genuine fun. Her huge mainsail and her wide decks covered with children have become a part of this landscape, and will stay part of it for generations.

There is nothing to do here but what the body wants, and so there is plenty. Generations come and go. The age of wealth and thoughtlessness is on its way, the age of ostentatious hull designs and high-speed fishing, the age of noise and social confusion and isolationism of the soul. All these things are coming into paradise. But right now I'm looking across the bay at the white steeple of the Melvin church, and at the volcanic Ossipees, and there is nothing out there on the water but the sunlit waves and a few floating yellow leaves with upturned stems.

The Hard Light

As soon as we had managed to take a few unsteady steps across the floor, my father figured it was time we learned to ski. He kept an old pair of wooden skis in the house, from which he had removed the edges. He strapped them onto our tiny feet and we clumped from room to room. By the time we were ready to hit the real slopes, a little later, we knew what we were supposed to do.

We were a skiing family. When the October wind blew up and the colored leaves flew from the trees, our eyes transformed them into snowflakes before they hit the ground. We didn't mind the air turning colder every day. We couldn't wait for the hard light of winter. Seven pairs of skis stood in a rack on the wall of the barn, waiting impatiently to break out of their blocks and head north.

Every Friday as soon as school was over, and at the beginning of every holiday, my parents directed seven of us with all our skis, poles boots, socks, underwear, parkas, hats, mittens and goggles into the car and we drove almost four hours north to my aunt and uncle's house in Norwich, Vermont, just across the frozen Connecticut River from the Dartmouth Skiway in Lyme, New Hampshire. This ski area, run by the college, was one of the most charming and idiosyncratic ski areas anywhere, and we routed it. Because we bought a season pass, and because we skied so decisively, it cost us about 50 cents a day to ski, and nothing, not even Christmas day, could stop us.

We slept like children, under the electric blankets on the soft beds in my aunt and uncle's large, comfortable house.

We woke up when the smell of bacon made it from the kitchen, around the corners and up the stairs to the bedrooms, and we jumped out of bed straight into our long underwear and stretch ski pants. The same crew of brothers and sisters and cousins that spent summers together at the lake, gathered around my aunt's kitchen table for cereal, orange juice, thick toast from her homemade bread, with homemade raspberry jam on top, bacon and eggs cooked to order. We thought all this was normal. From there we went straight into our cranky cars and off to the skiway, pulling our hats down over our ears while we watched our breaths inside the car.

We complained if any cars were parked ahead of us, and then we advanced to the lodge and mastered our boots in front of a roaring fire. We were almost always the first ones in line at the poma lift, getting there while it was still sputtering against the cold. We knew the trails so well, we could probably have skied them blindfolded. While we gamboled and sailed down the Gauntlet and Sachem and Lyme Drop, my mother did her careful "stem-cristies" down the nearly flat Papoose. But our favorite run was "Warden's Schuss." We skied down to the top of a section called the "Waterfall," which fully lived up to its name. We would dive off the top of this with a push, then get into a crouch and schuss the rest of the trail, five or more of us together, barely making the sharp corners and barely missing the other skiers who cluttered the lower slopes where a beginner's trail joined in. We put many lives in danger with every run.

We were good skiers and we knew it. Our only fault was our unimaginable hubris. The mountain belonged to us, and we helped wear it down. We felt like an elite group, because we all wore bright orange arm bands that made everyone look at us. Their real purpose was to be able to find each other. During the lonely trips up the mountain, my mind raced as fast as my skis on the way down. Every fantasy of childhood, every potential romance and every half-baked idea had time to play itself out before I reached the top of the mountain and started down again.

At noon, we converged at the back of a car. Ungloved hands gripped steaming cups of corn chowder served out of a huge cooker heated by a stone. There were crackers, and pickles and red faces, and laughter visibly surrounding us in the cold air. Gloves went on and we went back to our waiting skis, intending to make as many runs as humanly possible before the lifts closed in the late afternoon.

Then home to sleep and get up the next morning to do the same. This continued without pause for about twenty years. Odd days stuck out, like days of jumping and landing on top of people, days of skiing on rocks or into rivers, days of getting frostbite after every run, the day my father broke his leg trying to ski uphill, the day we had a wine flask and skied more in the woods than out, while one brother quoted Shakespeare to the trees.

Needless to say, we were building something more than our leg muscles all those years. We were adding a light of our own to winter's light, trying our best to reach the speed of light, to outdo fear and to humble winter. Strange how winter almost wraps the mind and the body in death, until you go out into it with others, and ski.

Where the Sweet Birds Sang

THAT TIME OF YEAR. YOU can see it in me. We have become the leaves, when few still hang in the trees. We are sweeping the shaggy grass inside the tall cedar hedge before our white house. From the end of our metal rakes comes a sound like the hiss of the sea blowing spume. It feels like we are cleaning house, as the leaves collect into huge jumping piles that dissipate, and grow again every day, and slowly make their way to the side of the road where one evening, after supper, near twilight, we will burn them.

The giant sugar maples won't mind the smoke rising through their empty arms toward the sky. The cedar hedge will be safe from the flames that only rise a little above the ground. The occasional car coming thoughtfully down the road will enjoy the small whiff of smoke that will find a way somehow into its lungs. We do this every year. My father directs us, with a rake in his hands that has a metal pipe for a handle.

He is joking around and rethinking the day out loud. Today he and my mother spent hours driving everywhere in the red pickup truck, looking for their car. It had been stolen out of our yard, but they were convinced they had left it and forgotten it somewhere, until finally the police returned it to us late in the afternoon.

I run to the house and sail back, crumpling a newspaper that has a picture of Kennedy on the front and a poem by Robert Frost on the back. I tuck it into the pile of leaves that stretches for twenty feet along the edge of the road. My brother Ted takes the matches from my father and leans down to light the paper. The paper ignites instantly. The leaves around it put out a thick blanket of smoke and then ignite too. The fire spreads through the pile and smoke fills the air and billows over the road.

We pull in more leaves with our rakes. The smell is rugged and soothing, unlike any other smell. The only thing it reminds me of is the pile of leaves burning the year before, and the year before that. It is a smell that threatens to turn acrid but never does. It is a gentle lyric that mounts to a rich music that permeates our clothes and hair, a happy, subtle spice that will stay on our bodies all night.

We can't stop pulling in the leaves. It's fun, something you don't ever want to end. Each leaf seems to release a thick incense that has been trapped beneath it just before it becomes a quick spurting flame and then turns instantly into a dark skeleton with tiny red veins shooting through it as swiftly as thought. Some leaves are outlined at their shrinking margins by these thin red lines, before they turn to a fine gray and white ash, as their neighbors are just beginning the same process.

Each leaf does its own smoke dance. Multiple legs of smoke, athletic and beautiful, twirl and rise and swirl into a larger crowd of legs going skyward. The dance turns to mysterious shapes in the twilight. Watching these shapes I fall into a kind of reverie and see the darkening world of my childhood turn into many worlds in front of me.

Look high and the smoke turns to a gray harmony at one with the twilight. But look close to the fire, and the tangling legs tell remarkable stories. There is the wizened face of Gram Perin, smiling at me. There is a knot of boys playing fox and geese. There is a giant, blue kite snaring itself in high branches. There are church steeples and young boys dancing with young girls, trying to grip balloons between their knees. There is the crooked stick of Uncle Elwood's dowsing rod.

There are my four brothers and my sister engaged in a million things, not one of them important, not one of them unimportant. There are scooters and skateboards, and games and songs and glasses clinking. There is music. There is the god of humor, dancing and dancing. There are days, weeks, decades, years, and dozens of lives and thousands of people. There is my father, and there is my mother. There are rock ledges blackened with water, cold streams with fishing lines coursing through them, granite boulders in every conceivable attitude, wild grape vines, dropped apples, and under them all, the golden trees.

This reverie has to end, though it just began. Death's second self is in the air, over the house and in the west. The fire that is glowing there will turn into the ashes of ourselves. We will be consumed with what nourished us.

I brush my teeth at the big bathroom sink and creep to my bed. I watch the strange lights that come off the head lamps of passing cars and make their way along the walls of my room. They rise up on one wall, pass over the ceiling or along the high part of another wall, and then set on the far wall. I know something from this, and from the smell of leaves that has crept into my room to stay with me. I know it without thinking it, without being able to think it. Our love is growing stronger by what we are leaving. Love it well, because you will be leaving it yourself before long.